Manual for
Theory and Practice
of Group Counseling

Manual for Theory and Practice of Group Counseling

SECOND EDITION

Gerald Corey
CALIFORNIA STATE UNIVERSITY, FULLERTON

Diplomate in Counseling Psychology
American Board of Professional Psychology

Brooks/Cole Publishing Company
Monterey, California

Brooks/Cole Publishing Company
A Division of Wadsworth, Inc.

Printed in the United States of America

10 9 8 7 6 5 4 3 2

ISBN 0-534-03428-4

Acquisition Editor: Claire Verduin
Production Coordinators: Louise Rixey/Ellen Brownstein
Cover Design: Vernon Boes
Typewriter Composition: Betty Ritter

Acknowledgments

I wish to extend my appreciation to my students at California State University at Fullerton, who used the material in this manual in the Practicum in Group Leadership. I have experimented with the exercises and activities in this revised manual with my classes for more than ten years in order to select the material that students find most meaningful.

Let me give special thanks and recognition to the following students who served as reviewers of the manual: Andrea Mark, Susan Gattis, Chuck Geddes, Larisa Lamb, Jan Davison, Bonnie Nelson, Randy Corliss, Donna Robbins, Diane Vasquez, and Merri Chalenor. The valuable suggestions of these students have increased the reading appeal and practicality of the manual. Kate McNamara of the Counseling Center of the University of Texas at Austin and Robert Cash of California State University at Long Beach also reviewed the manuscript and provided help in refining ideas.

Special thanks go to my wife (and colleague and friend), who helped devise many of the exercises and activities. I also am indebted to my close friends and colleagues for inspiration and challenge in developing the material presented. They are J. Michael Russell, Patrick Callanan, Helga Kennedy, and Mary Moline. We regularly co-lead groups and offer workshops, and the exercises that are presented have been applied to many groups. Our frequent conversations about group work and our actual work of leading groups as a team have kept my enthusiasm for groups high.

I invite you to express your ideas and your reactions to both this manual and the textbook, Theory and Practice of Group Counseling (second edition), by writing me at Brooks/Cole Publishing Company, Monterey, California, 93940. For your convenience, you can use the tear-out sheets provided at the end of the text and the manual. Your help will be appreciated.

Contents

PART ONE

Basic Elements of Group Process: An Overview

1

INTRODUCTION

This manual is designed to accompany <u>Theory and Practice of Group Coun-</u><u>seling</u> (second edition), by Gerald Corey (Brooks/Cole, 1985). The manual is intended to help you gain some practical experience in the various theoreti-cal approaches to group work, as well as to stimulate thought on basic ethi-cal and professional issues typically encountered by group leaders.

I hope the material in this manual will aid your own growth. Much of this material consists of things you can think about, experiment with, and do on your own; there are many exercises that you can practice in small groups, both as a leader and as a member. You'll be provided with opportu-nities to function in numerous role-playing situations, which can be very real and very instructive. I encourage you to modify these exercises so that they will become personally meaningful.

The design of the manual is based on the assumption that you will learn best by becoming actively involved in the learning process and by <u>actually</u> <u>experiencing</u> group concepts and techniques. Reading about them provides a foundation, yet this knowledge remains abstract unless you can see how these theories actually work in groups.

The exercise material includes:

1. self-inventories to assess your attitudes about various theories

2. open-ended questions for discussion and evaluation

3. ideas and suggestions for role playing

4. techniques for group interaction

5. practical problems that occur in groups

6. group exercises for experiential practice

7. suggestions of things you can do to apply what you are learning in the course to yourself personally and to yourself as a group leader.

There is more material in this manual than a given course can thoroughly cover. However, my preference is to provide a wide variety of questions and activities so that you can select the ones that you find most meaningful. The questions in this manual give a focus to your reading and will help you read and study in an active way.

HOW TO USE THE MANUAL AND THE TEXTBOOK

Below are some suggestions for getting the maximum value from the textbook and the manual. These suggestions are based on my experience in using the material in classes. My students have found the following guidelines to be of help in integrating and applying what they are studying.

1. First, I recommend looking over all the contents of the manual to get an overview of the course and the reading program.

2. Before you read and study a chapter in the textbook, read any summary material in the corresponding chapter in the manual, and then look over the Questions for Reflection and Discussion, if they are included in that chapter of the text. For the chapters that deal with theories of group counseling (part II), complete the manual's corresponding pre-chapter primer and self-inventory, which is based on the key concepts discussed in the textbook. Completing these self-inventories will help you determine the degree to which you agree or disagree with the concepts of a given theory. Taking these inventories and spending a few minutes reviewing them will give you a clearer focus on the chapter you're reading in the textbook.

3. After reading and studying the chapter in the textbook, return to the manual and do the following:

   a. If you have just finished a chapter on theory, retake or at least review the prechapter primer to see if your views have changed.

   b. For theoretical chapters, study the summary/overview charts that describe in brief form the developmental stages of a group, according to the particular theory.

   c. Look over the basic assumptions and summary of key concepts of the theory.

   d. Select some exercises to do on your own and some to do in a group.

4. Perhaps most important, get some actual experience in working in small classroom groups with the concepts and techniques of the various counseling approaches. The more you are willing to invest yourself in an active manner in small-group work, the more you'll be able to see the possibilities for actually using these techniques in groups you lead. Again, I have provided more small-group activities than can be done in even a two-hour self-directed group for training purposes. It is not expected that you will do all these exercises; your group should select several of them and experiment with them. In my course, in addition to the weekly seminars and class meetings in which we discuss the theory of group work, the students also meet in small experiential groups to gain practice in being a group member and in taking turns co-leading a group. At times, they work within the framework of the model we are studying in class, and in this way they get a better idea of how therapies are

actually applied in a group. The students _experience_ the problems involved in making the translation from theory to practice, they find out what aspects of each theory they want to incorporate into their style of group leadership, and they learn by interacting with their peers. You are encouraged to use your ingenuity with the exercises that are presented. Use them as a springboard for developing your own exercises. Think of different ways that you might use the techniques you learn in the group you lead.

5. _Theory and Practice in Group Counseling_ is designed as a survey textbook, and, as such, it can't provide an advanced and detailed treatment of the theories presented. My aim is to introduce you to some of the key concepts of a variety of theories underlying group practice and to describe some of the therapeutic techniques that flow from these concepts. I hope that, when you finish studying the textbook and manual, you will want to read more about some of the therapies. Following each chapter on theory is an annotated list of recommended supplementary reading that will give you additional information.

6. The manual is designed as a guide and a resource to help you eventually create your own theory and style of group leading. Toward this end, I recommend that, as you read and study the textbook and manual, you look for both the characteristics shared by the approaches and the major differences among them, determine the unique characteristics of each model, and select specific aspects of each approach that appear to be suited to your personality. The manual's main purpose is to make these theories and issues come alive to you. To accomplish this it is essential that you involve yourself actively by thinking critically, share your thoughts with others in class, and invest yourself emotionally by bringing your own life experience into this program.

7. As you read and study the textbook and the manual, be alert for topics for class discussion and topics that most interest you. Write down a few key questions and bring them to class. Look for concepts and techniques that you can apply to the group you are leading or expect to be leading. As you read and work through the material, develop a capacity for critical evaluation by thinking about what you most like and least like about each of the theories.

8. I strongly recommend that you read Chapters 16 and 17 ("Illustration of a Group in Action" and "Comparisons, Contrasts, and Integration") _early_. They will provide you with a case illustration of themes typically explored in groups, with ways various theories can be applied to a group, and with a cognitive map to help you see similarities and differences among the ten theories in the book.

2

ETHICAL AND PROFESSIONAL ISSUES
IN GROUP PRACTICE

A SELF-INVENTORY OF YOUR VIEWS ON ETHICAL PRACTICE IN GROUP WORK

This inventory is designed to stimulate your thinking about what constitutes ethical practice in the leading of groups. I suggest that you take the inventory before you study the guidelines for group leaders developed by the Association for Specialists in Group Work (ASGW), which follow in this chapter of the manual. I have found it a good practice to have students form small groups to compare their reactions to the statements in the inventory. Later in this chapter there are exercises and activities and a second self-inventory, all of which provide material for reflection and lively discussion in class.

In taking this first self-inventory, decide for each item the degree to which you think the leader's behavior is proper or improper, using the following code:

1 = This behavior is <u>illegal</u>.

2 = This behavior is <u>clearly unethical</u>.

3 = This behavior is <u>borderline</u>. A judgment would depend on the particulars of the situation.

4 = This behavior is <u>ethical</u>.

5 = This behavior is <u>clinically inappropriate</u>.

<u>Note</u>: You may want to use more than one response. For example, you may want to rate an item with both numbers 1 and 2. And you might also have your own reaction to an item besides one of the five listed above. Bring any of your reactions to class to compare your ideas with others.

_5_   1.   The leader conducts an intensive weekend group and does not make any provision for a follow-up session.

_2_   2.   The leader continues to lead groups even though claiming to be extremely tired of group work (and not really believing it to be of therapeutic value).

_1_   3.   The leader makes tapes of the group sessions without the knowledge and consent of the members, based on the rationale that telling them would inhibit their free participation.

_3_   4.   The leader does not screen prospective members, mainly on the ground that members will screen themselves out of a group if they find that it is not appropriate for them.

_3_   5.   The leader refuses to see members between sessions, even if they request such a private session, and instead asks them to bring up the issue at the next group meeting.

_2_   6.   The leader makes it a practice to go on dates with members of the group, stating that this does not inhibit one's capacity to work effectively with members.

_5_   7.   The leader fails to intervene when several members gang up on another member and pressure that person to make a decision.

_1+2_   8.   The leader introduces techniques in a group, even though he or she has not been trained in the use of these techniques, but does so thinking that this is the best way to learn.

_2_   9.   The leader does not discuss with members any personal risks associated with joining a group, on the ground that one should not give members any fears that they might not already have.

_2_   10.   The group leader does not mention confidentiality, thinking that if this topic is important, members will eventually bring it up.

_2_   11.   The leader consciously attempts to push personal agendas and values on group members.

_2_   12.   The leader sees nothing wrong in influencing the group in a subtle manner to accept his or her values.

_2_   13.   The leader conducts groups in order to get personal needs met through this work.

_2_   14.   The group leader plays favorites and does not strive to treat all members equally.

_2_   15.   The group leader fosters the dependence of the members.

_1+2_   16.   The leader initiates sexual relationships with certain members, stating that this practice is not harmful because the clients are consenting adults.

5   17. The leader allows one member to dominate the group and does not intervene when this member rambles on and monopolizes the group's time.

5   18. The leader ignores the fact that a member comes to the sessions under the influence of drugs.

1+2   19. The group leader is conducting research that involves the group but does not disclose this fact to the members.

5   20. The leader pushes clients to make decisions.

2+5   21. The leader does not provide any written statements about his or her qualifications, the purpose of the group, or the procedures to be employed.

5   22. The leader does not state what services will be provided within the structure of the group.

1+2   23. The leader allows the expression of pent-up rage in group sessions but does not take precautions to see that members are not physically injured in these exercises.

2+5   24. The leader coerces members to participate in nonverbal touching exercises, thinking that this type of pressure is needed if they are to challenge their inhibitions.

2+5   25. The leader presses members to experience intense emotions and pushes for a catharsis—even if they say they do not want to explore a struggle—out of the conviction that they need to experience their emotions to become free.

5 2   26. The leader does not allow a member to leave the room.

2+5   27. The leader does not explain a technique that the group will be using and does not give the members a choice whether to participate in this technique.

2+5   28. When confidentiality is broken in a group of high school students, the leader ignores the situation, assuming that to discuss the matter or to take action will make things worse.

1+2   29. The leader forms a group with elementary school children without getting parental permission.

2+5   30. The group leader discusses in some detail his or her own involvement with drugs, thinking that this will promote openness and trust among a group of adolescents.

ASGW ETHICAL AND TRAINING GUIDELINES

The following documents, Ethical Guidelines for Group Leaders, and Professional Standards for Training of Group Counselors, were developed by the Association for Specialists in Group Work (ASGW) for use by its members. Interested persons who wish to join the ASGW, a division of the American Association for Counseling and Development, should write to:

President
Association for Specialists in Group Work
5999 Stevenson Avenue
Alexandria, VA 22304

In my classes I have students form small groups to discuss and evaluate the guidelines. Each group presents its conclusions to the entire class. We focus on the issues that seem to generate the greatest degree of controversy. My students have argued with some of the points, thought that certain guidelines were incomplete, and found that modifications (expansions or deletions) were needed in some cases.

Guidelines such as these should be continually evaluated and refined. The guidelines are comprehensive and represent many months of collective thought and discussion, and I think they provide some direction for group workers in developing a sense of professionalism.

Study the following guidelines and mark the items that interest you most. Bring these items to class for discussion and debate. What ethical guidelines do you think are most important? What guidelines, if any, do you disagree with? Are there any guidelines that should be added to this document? What are your reactions to the guidelines for training group leaders? How do these standards of training in clinical group practice compare with your own views of training and your own experience in being trained as a group leader?

ETHICAL GUIDELINES FOR GROUP LEADERS*

Preamble

One characteristic of any professional group is the possession of a body of knowledge and skills and mutually acceptable ethical standards for putting them into practice. Ethical standards consist of those principles which have been formally and publicly acknowledged by the membership of a profession to serve as guidelines governing professional conduct, discharge of duties, and resolution of moral dilemmas. In this document, the Association for Specialists in Group Work has identified the standards of conduct necessary to maintain and regulate the high standards of integrity and leadership among its members.

The Association for Specialists in Group Work recognizes the basic commitment of its members to the Ethical Standards of its parent organization, the American Association for Counseling and Development, and nothing in this document shall be construed to supplant that code. These standards are intended to complement the AACD standards in the area of group work by clarify-

---

*Ethical Guidelines for Group Leaders (1980 revision). Approved by the ASGW Executive Board, November 11, 1980. Reprinted by permission.

ing the nature of ethical responsibility of the counselor in the group setting and by stimulating a greater concern for competent group leadership.

The following ethical guidelines have been organized under three categories: the leader's responsibility for providing information about group work to clients, the leader's responsibility for providing group counseling services to clients, and the leader's responsibility for safeguarding the standards of ethical practice.

A. **Responsibility for Providing Information about Group Work and Group Services:**

A-1. Group leaders shall fully inform group members, in advance and preferably in writing, of the goals in the group, qualifications of the leader, and procedures to be employed.

A-2. The group leader shall conduct a pre-group interview with each prospective member for purposes of screening and orientation and, insofar as possible, shall select group members whose needs and goals are compatible with the established goals of the group; who will not impede the group process; and whose well-being will not be jeopardized by the group experience.

A-3. Group leaders shall protect members by defining clearly what confidentiality means, why it is important, and the difficulties involved in enforcement.

A-4. Group leaders shall explain, as realistically as possible, exactly what services can and cannot be provided within the particular group structure offered.

A-5. Group leaders shall provide prospective clients with specific information about any specialized or experimental activities in which they may be expected to participate.

A-6. Group leaders shall stress the personal risks involved in any group, especially regarding potential life-changes, and help group members explore their readiness to face these risks.

A-7. Group leaders shall inform members that participation is voluntary and that they may exit from the group at any time.

A-8. Group leaders shall inform members about recording of sessions and how tapes will be used.

B. **Responsibility for Providing Group Services to Clients:**

B-1. Group leaders shall protect member rights against physical threats, intimidation, coercion, and undue peer pressure.

B-2. Group leaders shall refrain from imposing their own agendas, needs, and values on group members.

B-3. Group leaders shall insure that each member has the opportunity to utilize group resources and interact within the group by minimizing barriers such as rambling and monopolizing time.

B-4. Group leaders shall treat each member individually and equally.

B-5. Group leaders shall abstain from inappropriate personal relationships with members throughout the duration of the group and any subsequent professional involvement.

9

B-6. Group leaders shall help promote independence of members from the group in the most efficient period of time.

B-7. Group leaders shall not attempt any technique unless thoroughly trained in its use or under supervision by an expert familiar with the intervention.

B-8. Group leaders shall not condone the use of alcohol or drugs directly prior to or during group sessions.

B-9. Group leaders shall make every effort to assist clients in developing their personal goals.

B-10. Group leaders shall provide between-session consultation to group members and follow-up after termination of the group, as needed or requested.

C. Responsibility for Safeguarding Ethical Practice:

C-1. Group leaders shall display these standards or make them available to group members.

C-2. Group leaders have the right to expect ethical behavior from colleagues and are obligated to rectify or disclose incompetent, unethical behavior demonstrated by a colleague by taking the following actions:

a. To confront the individual with the apparent violation of ethical guidelines for the purpose of protecting the safety of any clients and to help the group leader correct any inappropriate behaviors.

b. Such a complaint should be made in writing including the specific facts and dates of the alleged violation and all relevant supporting data. The complaints should be forwarded to:

> The Ethics Committee,
> c/o The President
> Association for Specialists in
>   Group Work
> 5999 Stevenson Avenue
> Alexandria, VA 22304

The envelope must be marked "CONFIDENTIAL" in order to assure confidentiality for both the accuser(s) and the alleged violator(s). Upon receipt, the President shall (a) check on membership status of the charged member(s), (b) confer with legal counsel, and (c) send the case with all pertinent documents to the chairperson of the ASGW Ethics Committee within ten (10) working days after receipt of the complaint.

c. If it is determined by the Ethics and Professional Standards Committee that the alleged breach of ethical conduct constitutes a violation of the "Ethical Guidelines," then an investigation will be started within ten (10) days by at least one member of the Committee plus two additional ASGW members in the locality of the alleged violation. The investigating committee chairperson shall: (a) acknowledge receipt of the complaint, (b) review the complaint and supporting data, (c) send a letter of acknowledgment to the member(s) of the complaint regarding alleged violations along with a request for a response and relevant information related to the complaint, and (d) inform members of the Ethics Committee by letter of the case and present a plan of action for investigation.

d. All information, correspondence, and activities of the Ethics Committee will remain confidential. It shall be determined that no person serving as an investigator on a case have any disqualifying relationship with the alleged violator(s).

e. The charged party(ies) will have not more than 30 days in which to answer the charges in writing. The charged party(ies) will have free access to all cited evidence from which to make a defense, including the right to legal counsel and a formal hearing before the ASGW Ethics Committee.

f. Based upon the investigation of the Committee and any designated local ASGW members one of the following recommendations may be made to the Executive Board for appropriate action:

1. Advise that the charges be dropped.
2. Reprimand and admonishment against repetition of the charged conduct.
3. Notify the charged member(s) of his/her right to a formal hearing before the ASGW Ethics Committee, and request a response to be made to the Ethics Chairperson as to his/her decision on the matter. Such hearing would be conducted in accordance with the AACD Policy and Procedures for Processing Complaints of Ethical Violations, "Procedures for Hearings," and would be scheduled for a time coinciding with the annual AACD convention. Conditions for such hearing shall also be in accordance with the AACD Policy and Procedures document, "Options Available to the Ethics Committee, item 3."
4. Suspension of membership for a specified period from ASGW.
5. Dismissal from membership in ASGW.

PROFESSIONAL STANDARDS FOR TRAINING OF GROUP COUNSELORS*

Preamble

Whereas counselors may be able to function effectively with individual clients, they are also required to possess specialized knowledge and skills that render them effective in group counseling. The Association for Specialists in Group Work supports the preparation of group practitioners as part of and in addition to counselor education.

---

*These Professional Standards for Training of Group Counselors were developed by the Association for Specialists in Group Work and approved by the ASGW Executive Board on March 20, 1983. The group counselor knowledge competencies and skill competencies are reprinted by permission of the ASGW. (Note: The rating scale is an adaptation of the printed standards, done for the purpose of helping the users of this manual make a self-assessment of their own level of competency as a group leader.)

The <u>Professional Standards for Training of Group Counselors</u> represent the minimum core of group leader (cognitive and applied) competencies that have been identified by the Association for Specialists in Group Work.

Designated Group Counseling Areas

In order to work as a professional in Group Counseling, an individual must meet and demonstrate minimum competencies in the generic core of group counseling standards. These are applicable to all training programs regardless of level of work or specialty area. In addition to the genetic core competencies (and in order to practice in a specific area of expertise), the individual will be required to meet one or more specialty area standards (school counseling and guidance, student personnel services in higher education, or community/mental health agency counseling).

<u>Directions</u>: Rate yourself on the following competencies, using this scale:

     5 = I am especially strong in this competency.

     4 = I am very high to good in this competency.

     3 = I am just adequate and could surely improve.

     2 = I am weak, deficient, and needing much improvement.

     1 = I am especially lacking in this competency.

The qualified group leader has demonstrated specialized knowledge in the following aspects of group work:

_____ 1. Be able to state for at least three major theoretical approaches to group counseling the distinguishing characteristics of each and the commonalities shared by all.

_____ 2. Basic principles of group dynamics and the therapeutic ingredients of groups.

_____ 3. Personal characteristics of group leaders that have an impact on members; knowledge of personal strengths, weaknesses, biases, values and their impact on others.

_____ 4. Specific ethical problems and considerations unique to group counseling.

_____ 5. Body of research on group counseling in one's specialty area (school counseling, college student personnel, or community/ mental health agency).

_____ 6. Major modes of group work, differentiation among the modes, and the appropriate instances in which each is used (such as group guidance, group counseling, group therapy, human relations training, etc.).

_____ 7. Process components involved in typical stages of a group's development (i.e., characteristics of group interaction and counselor roles).

_____ 8. Major facilitative and debilitative roles that group members may take.

_____ 9. Advantages and disadvantages of group counseling and the circumstances for which it is indicated or contraindicated.

Group Counselor Skill Competencies

The qualified group leader has shown the following abilities:

_____ 1. To screen and assess readiness levels of prospective clients.

_____ 2. To deliver a clear, concise, and complete definition of group counseling.

_____ 3. To recognize self-defeating behaviors of group members.

_____ 4. To describe and conduct a personally selected group counseling model appropriate to the age and clientele of the group leader's specialty area(s).

_____ 5. To accurately identify nonverbal behavior among group members.

_____ 6. To exhibit appropriate pacing skills involved in stages of a group's development.

_____ 7. To identify and intervene effectively at critical incidents in the group process.

_____ 8. To appropriately work with disruptive group members.

_____ 9. To make use of the major strategies, techniques, and procedures of group counseling.

_____ 10. To provide and use procedures to assist transfer and support of changes by group members in the natural environment.

_____ 11. To use adjunct group structures such as psychological homework (i.e., self-monitoring, contracting).

_____ 12. To use basic group leader interventions such as process comments, empathic responses, self-disclosure, confrontations, etc.

_____ 13. To facilitate therapeutic conditions and forces in group counseling.

_____ 14. To work cooperatively and effectively with a co-leader.

_____ 15. To open and close sessions, and terminate the group process.

_____ 16. To provide follow-up procedures to assist maintenance and support of group members.

_____ 17. To utilize assessment procedures in evaluating effects and contributions of group counseling.

Training in Clinical Practice

Type of Supervised Experience	Minimum Number of Clock Hours Required: Master's or Entry Level Program
1. Critique of group tapes (by self or others)	5
2. Observing group counseling (live or media presentation)	5
3. Participating as a member in a group	15
4. Leading a group with a partner and receiving critical feedback from a supervisor	15
5. Practicum: Leading a group alone, with critical self-analysis of performance; supervisor feedback on tape; and self-analysis	15
6. Fieldwork of Internship: Practice as a group leader with on-the-job supervision	25

EVALUATING GROUP-LEADERSHIP COMPETENCIES

1. Look over your ratings on the 26 group-counselor knowledge and skill competencies to get a sense of your current level of proficiency. What do you think you can do to develop those areas where you are weak? Form small groups in class to discuss your self-ratings. As a group, what ideas can you come up with to develop and maintain each of the knowledge and skill competencies?

2. Carefully look at the ASGW's recommendations for <u>training in clinical practice</u>. What do you think about the scope of the types of supervised experience (and number of hours for specific experiences) that are suggested? What training in group work have you received to date? What supervised group experiences have you had so far? What experiences do you expect to have by the time you complete your program? Again, form small groups in class and discuss the ASGW's suggestions and the types of supervised experiences you deem essential. You might also discuss ways in which you can continue to develop group-leadership skills once you complete your program of studies.

EXERCISES AND ACTIVITIES

The following situations in groups are presented for your analysis and for class discussion. Consider these cases in light of the ethical guidelines discussed in the chapter. What do you see as the ethical issues in each situation? To what degree do you think that the group leader in each situation acted in an ethical or unethical manner? What do you think you would have done differently? How might the situation in each case be remedied? Do you have any thoughts pertaining to how an unethical practice might have been avoided? The object of these exercises is to give you practice in ethical decision making and an opportunity to discuss ethical issues involved in the practice of group work.

Read each of the case situations presented and respond by putting the number that best represents your opinion about the group leader's behavior:

    1 = unethical

    2 = somewhat unethical

    3 = uncertain

    4 = somewhat ethical

    5 = ethical

_____ 1. <u>Informed consent</u>. The leader of a group in a state mental hospital takes great care to inform the members of their rights, of the procedures to be used, and of all the factors that could influence their participation in the group. She does so on the ground that groups are a mandatory form of therapy in the hospital, and she believes that extreme care should be taken so that their rights are not violated. However, for the clients in her private practice, who seek a group voluntarily, she does not see it as important to secure their written permission, nor does she explain in much detail what they are about to commit themselves to. Her rationale is that these clients will be more likely to create their own norms if she avoids providing any information beyond the minimum.

Do you agree with her rationale and approach for each type of group? Do you think that she should provide as much information to clients in her private practice as she does to those in the institution? Specifically, what might you want to tell a prospective member about a group? How much detailed information would you think it optimal to provide?

_____ 2. <u>Screening</u>. A group for adults is offered in a community mental-health center. The leader makes the assumption that, if the members have adequate information about a group, they will be able to determine for themselves if the group is appropriate for their purposes. She makes no provisions for screening members individually and asks the secretary to fill the group with the first ten people who ask to join, providing that they have read the material that she has provided for people considering the group.

Do you think that providing adequate information to prospective clients is an appropriate substitute for screening people on an individual basis? What are some advantages and disadvantages of this group leader's approach? Do you think that screening individuals for a group is always essential? Why or why not? Can you think of cases in which you might <u>not</u> screen? What are some alternatives to screening if this process is not practical?

_____ 3. <u>Confidentiality</u>. In an adolescent group in a community clinic, several members disclose their illegal involvement with drug traffic in their high school, including selling drugs to fellow students. At the outset of this group, the leader did discuss confidentiality and the legal restrictions of keeping and breaking confidences. He mentioned that he would have to divulge confidential disclosures if they involved illegal actions or if he felt that a client might be a harm to self or others. When this disclosure pertaining to drugs is made, however, the leader tells the group that he will keep what has been said in the group, because he does not want to take any action that might damage the trust level of the group.

What are your reactions to this leader's course of action? If you were the leader in this situation, what do you think you might do? Do you think the leader should have reported the matter, even at the risk of affecting the trust in the group? Under what specific conditions might you feel compelled to divulge something that you found out in the course of a group?

_____ 4. <u>Scope of services</u>. The group leader tells the members that she is available for individual consultations with members between group sessions. A young man sees her for a private session and tells her of his extreme lack of comfort in the group. He says he simply does not trust several of the members. When the leader encourages him to bring this matter up in the group, he firmly declares that he does not intend to. He says he is unwilling at this time to make the same disclosures in the group that he has made in private with her. She agrees to keep the matter confidential.

What are the advantages and disadvantages of providing members with the opportunity to have private sessions if they feel a need for them at certain times? Would you have agreed to keep what this client told you confidential, or would you have insisted that he discuss the issue in a group session? What ethical issues are involved either way you might decide?

_____ 5. <u>Experimental activities</u>. As a part of a doctoral study, a group leader is using certain experimental procedures in various groups as a part of his internship in a community clinic. He decides not to inform the members of any of his groups that he is conducting a study, for three reasons: he does not want them to feel as if they are being experimented upon; he does not want to pollute the nature of the experiment; and he does not want the members to think that he is not fully trained and experienced. Therefore, he not only does not tell them about the experimental activities but also fails to mention that he is doing these groups as a part of his doctoral internship.

16

Is he being unethical in keeping both facts from his clients? How would you address the concerns that led him to withhold information? If you were in this situation, what might you tell the members of your group? What would you not tell them?

_____ 6. Risks in groups. A group leader deliberately avoids bringing up any potential risks during the early sessions of her group. She is concerned that, if she mentions psychological risks, members may become needlessly agitated. She makes the choice not to help members determine their readiness to face any potential life changes that might come about as a result of participating in the group.

What are the ethics of this situation? What risks might you want to discuss with members? How would you help clients determine their readiness to face certain risks in a group?

_____ 7. Freedom of exit. At the first group session the leader asks for a commitment from the members to remain in the group for the full 20 weeks. He says that, if members leave before the group terminates, it is likely to damage the cohesion of the group as well as contributing to unfinished business. He says: "If you decide to join this group and return next week, I expect you to finish this group. If you have any thoughts to the contrary, please do not return next week."

Do you think it is ethical to demand that members remain in a group until it terminates? Do you believe that ethical practice implies that members have the freedom to leave a group at any time? How would you handle this issue? Are there any alternatives? What problems do you see in situations where members drop out?

_____ 8. Tape-recording group sessions. A student group leader who is being supervised makes tape recordings of sessions with the permission of the members. However, the leader does not tell them that some tapes are likely to be played in her supervision group. Her reason is that she does not want to contribute to some members' being self-conscious and monitoring what they say in sessions.

Is this leader unethical in failing to tell the members that others might listen to the tapes? If you were this student and were asked by your supervisor to tape-record, how would you deal with the situation in your group? What would you say to the members?

_____ 9. Coercion and pressure. The members of a group are told by the leader that he intends to use peer pressure and coercive tactics to get them to make changes in their life. He states his belief that both peer pressure and leader pressure are healthy for promoting movement in a group and leading to changed behavior outside of the group. The leader warns them that he will make definite use of pressure as a therapeutic leverage.

Since the members are forewarned, do you see any ethical issues in this case? Do you think that coercion can be therapeutic? Or do you think that it is counterproductive? What kind of pressure, if any, would you see as acceptable? Can you give an example of "undue pressure" that you consider unethical?

_____ 10. Imposing leader values. A group leader says that he makes it a general rule to try to keep his values hidden. If members ask him what his views are on controversial issues, he tells them that he makes it a practice not to disclose his values because he does not want to influence members to think and decide in line with his values.

First of all, how possible do you think it is that you can keep your values from members in a group that you are leading? Are you less likely to impose your values by keeping them to yourself or by sharing them when appropriate? What difference do you see between imposing and exposing your values? Do you see it as your function as a leader to challenge the values of members? What ways can you see yourself influencing your group to adopt your values or to think as you do?

_____ 11. Personal relationships. A group leader accepts a social invitation from the members of his group. The group occasionally meets for a party, and the members thought it would be good to invite the leader so they could get to know him better outside of the formal relationship and the office. He accepts and goes to their party.

How wise do you think it is for a leader to be involved in any social activities with members outside of the group? Can you think of when and in what circumstances you might accept such an offer, if at all? What are the possible advantages of being a part of such activities? What about the possible disadvantages? When, if at all, do you think that having personal relationships with members becomes an ethical issue?

_____ 12. Use of techniques. A leader uses body-oriented and other techniques designed to induce catharsis. He has not had specialized training or supervision in these techniques (even though he has had supervised training in group work). He uses these techniques on the ground that he can learn how to apply them skillfully only with actual practice. He contends that, since he experienced some intensive techniques as a member of a group, he has some direction.

Do you think this leader is unethical? Why or why not? How do you determine when you are sufficiently trained in a given technique? What kinds of technique might you avoid? Does the kind of group you have make a difference in the techniques you will employ?

_____ 13. Training as a group leader. A licensed counselor forms a weekly group in her private practice, even though she has not had specific training as a group counselor. Most of her course work and most of her supervised experience were in individual counseling, and she had only one basic course in group counseling (with no actual opportunity to lead groups under supervision).

Since she has not had specific training and supervision as a group counselor, is she being ethical in organizing a group without supervision? Do you think the skills she learned in individual counseling will enable her to lead a group alone? If you wanted to form a group and did not have the specific background in group work, what might you do? How would you be able to tell when you were competent to lead a group by yourself?

_____ 14. Alcohol and drugs. The leader of an adolescent group is aware that a member attends some of the sessions under the influence of drugs. Rather than dealing with him in the group, the leader sees him privately and confronts him with her suspicion. He agrees that he has come to several sessions "loaded," because it makes the sessions more bearable and helps him let go of some of the anxiety that he feels in the group. She asks him to bring up this matter in the next group, because she thinks he is using drugs as an escape. She also tells him of her concern about the legal ramifications of attending her group "loaded."

What do you think of the manner in which the leader deals with this client? What ground rules would you establish regarding the use of alcohol or drugs directly before or during the group sessions? What might you do if you were quite certain that several adolescents were attending the group meetings under the influence of some type of drug? What legal and ethical issues do you see involved?

_____ 15. Follow-up after termination. A weekend marathon personal-growth group is scheduled. Although members are screened briefly before being admitted, once the group terminates, there will be no more contact with the leader, individually or in a group. No follow-up sessions are scheduled because the leader lives in another state, and he sees follow-up as impractical.

Do you think that ethical practice demands a follow-up session after a group is over? What dangers, if any, do you see in the marathon group described above? What alternatives do you see in this leader's case, since he lives in another state? What kind of follow-up procedures would you like to make a part of any group that you lead?

Once you have thought through the issues, jot down your ideas and bring them to class. These short vignettes provide excellent material for getting you and your fellow students thinking about the application of ethical standards to the practice of group work. It is best not to think simply in terms of "right" and "wrong," but rather to try to formulate a course of action that seems responsible in each of the cases. When you discuss these situations in small groups in class, be sure to give the reasons behind your views.

A SELF-INVENTORY TO EVALUATE ETHICAL DECISION MAKING
AND REVIEW BASIC ISSUES

The following multiple choice self-inventory is presented as a device for clarifying your thinking on various ethical issues, most of which relate to the ASGW ethical guidelines. Now that you have studied and discussed the cases and the ASGW guidelines, this inventory can serve as an excellent basis for review, can provide material for lively class discussions, and can give you additional practice in the process of ethical decision making. Keep in mind that there are no "right answers"; this inventory is designed to stimulate thought and to help you formulate your own positions on many of the ethical and professional issues that you are likely to encounter as a group practitioner.

After you complete this inventory, note the items that produced the strongest responses in you and bring them up in class for further discussion. Use this inventory in any way that you can to stimulate debate in your class.

Circle the letter beside the response that most clearly reflects your viewpoint at this time. Circle as many responses as you wish; if you don't like any of the responses provided, write your own response on the blank line.

1. What is unethical behavior on the part of a group leader?

    a. any actions that are contrary to the established codes of the ASGW
    b. anything that harms a member or is not in the best interests of the member.
    c. behavior that the leader judges to be unethical
    d. meeting personal needs at the expense of the members
    e. _____

2. Under what conditions would you break confidentiality?

    a. only when I would be obliged to legally
    b. if I believed my client would harm himself or herself
    c. if I were frightened for my own safety
    d. if I found out that a member was engaging in unlawful actions
    e. _____

3. What criteria would you use to decide when to break confidentiality?

    a. consultation with my colleagues
    b. trusting my own intuitions
    c. seeking direction from a supervisor
    d. following the policy of the agency I worked for
    e. _____

4. What is your view of sexual intimacy between a member and a leader of a group?

    a. It is always unethical.
    b. Under some circumstances it could be beneficial for some members.
    c. It is an exploitation of the member, and it hurts the person.
    d. It is impossible effectively to combine a sexual relationship with a therapeutic one.
    e. _____

5. What is your position on the issue of leaders' having social relationships with members?

    a. It is unethical and unprofessional.
    b. It strictly depends on the leader to make the judgment whether it would interfere with therapy.
    c. It could be useful to build trust and a good therapeutic relationship.
    d. It depends on the group member.
    e. _____

6. What is your view of nonerotic physical contact with clients?

    a. It is dangerous and can easily lead to overt sexual behavior.
    b. It can be very useful therapeutically.
    c. There are more disadvantages than advantages.
    d. It is useful only if it is genuine on the leader's part.
    e. _____

7. What criteria would you use to develop your own professional code of ethics?

    a. I'd rely on the established codes and standards.
    b. I'd do whatever felt right and appropriate to me.
    c. I'd discuss questions and issues with colleagues I trusted.
    d. I'd discuss any questionable behaviors with group members.
    e. _____

8. Which of the following measures best determine a group leader's level of competence?

    a. possession of a license or credential as a mental-health practitioner
    b. completion of broad course work in the theory and practice of group counseling
    c. supervised practice in group work
    d. affiliation with a professional organization
    e. _____

9. What do you think about a group leader who does not inform members of the procedures and techniques that will be a part of the group process?

    a. This leader is behaving unethically.
    b. It all depends on the type of group.
    c. It depends on the theoretical stance of the leader.
    d. It is not wise, but it is not unethical.
    e. _____

10. How essential do you consider a pregroup interview with each prospective member to be?

    a. Leaders who fail to conduct them are unethical.
    b. Sometimes it is simply not practical to do so.
    c. There are other alternatives that can be used when pregroup interviews are not practical or possible.
    d. Pregroup interviews are generally not necessary.
    e. _____

11. What is your view of screening members for a group?

    a. Ethical practice demands it.
    b. Generally, it is a waste of time.
    c. In screening, it is important for the leader to rely upon his or her own judgment about including or excluding a member.
    d. Screening should be a two-way process.
    e. _____

12. How would you determine whether members are benefiting from a group?

    a. I'd ask them if they were benefiting from the sessions.
    b. I'd give certain tests.
    c. I'd look to evidence of behavioral changes outside of the group.
    d. I'd rely upon my judgement.
    e. _____

13. What criterion would you use to determine whether you were competent to work with certain kinds of group members?

    a. I'd let the client decide.
    b. I would rely upon my own judgment.
    c. If I had a license, then I'd be competent.
    d. I'd let my supervisor or boss decide for me.
    e. _____

14. What is your view of group pressure (when several members in a group apply pressure to another member)?

    a. It's unethical.
    b. It's a good way to break down defenses and make progress.
    c. Group pressure is a basic part of any group.
    d. The leader's task is to see that members are never pressured.
    e. _____

15. What is your view of members' socializing outside of the group?

    a. I am opposed to it, because therapy and social life don't mix well.
    b. I think it can make a group more like real life.
    c. It depends on the effect it has on the group.
    d. It depends on the population that makes up the group.
    e. _____

16. What steps would you take to protect the group's confidentiality?

    a. I'd get members to sign a contract agreeing not to talk about group matters outside of sessions.
    b. I would tape-record all sessions.
    c. I would often bring up the topic for discussion.
    d. I'd let the group take care of this matter.
    e. _____

17. What professional responsibility do you think group leaders have to demonstrate the effectiveness of their groups?

    a. Ethical practice demands some attempt to study the outcomes.
    b. It is almost impossible to determine adequately whether a group is effective.
    c. It is a member's responsibility to participate in research.
    d. Leaders should design a research program to determine the level of effectiveness of their groups.
    e. _____

18. How professional or ethical do you think it is for a group leader to occasionally use group time to discuss and explore his or her own personal problems in the group?

    a. This is almost always unwise and unprofessional.
    b. Any time leaders take the focus off members, they are behaving un-ethically.
    c. This kind of behavior means that the person is not ready to lead groups.

d. This can be a useful way to model, and it can actually make the leader more effective.

e. _____

19. Should a group leader expect members to take an active part in all of the group exercises?

a. Group members should always be free to decline to participate in any activity.

b. If members join a group, they should go along with all of its activities.

c. Leaders can insist on uniform participation, for if everyone does not participate, it will hurt the morale and trust level.

d. If members decide not to participate in an exercise, they should state their reasons for not wanting to participate.

e. _____

20. What is your position on using structured exercises in groups?

a. They are best avoided, because they tend to foster member dependency on the leader.

b. They can be useful catalysts to interaction.

c. They should be used only if leaders have a rationale for them.

d. They should be used when the group begins to lose vitality.

e. _____

21. What is your view of providing private sessions to members between sessions, if they request such a service?

a. I'd encourage this practice.

b. I'd discourage this practice.

c. I think that doing so would get in the way of developing group cohesion.

d. I'd urge the member to bring up the issue at the next group session.

e. _____

22. If you were leading a group of minors, would you secure written parental permission?

a. Yes, because it is legally sound to do so.

b. Yes, because it is ethically the appropriate course of action.

c. Yes, because it is politically wise.

d. No, because it is not necessary.

e. _____

23. What comes closest to your view on the professional responsibility of a leader to provide some type of follow-up session, once a group ends?

a. It is clearly unethical to fail to offer a follow-up session.

b. This matter should be left for the group members to decide.

c. It could actually foster a dependent attitude on the members' part.

d. It could easily be a way for the group leader to avoid dealing with his or her feelings of separation after termination of the group.

e. _____

24. What is your position on the guideline stating that members may exit from the group at any time?

    a. I fully support this concept.
    b. I disagree; once a member makes a commitment to the group, he or she should honor this commitment.
    c. I would make it very difficult for a member simply to exit.
    d. At the very least, I'd want the member to discuss his or her reason for considering leaving the group.
    e. _____

25. What are your views of tape-recording group sessions?

    a. My hope is that members would want their sessions taped.
    b. I might consider tape-recording sessions without their permission if I felt that they would be unspontaneous.
    c. I would get written permission before using any recorder.
    d. I would encourage members to listen to the tapes after the session.
    e. _____

26. Which of the following comes closest to your viewpoint?

    a. It is the leader's function to teach values in a group.
    b. Leaders should clearly state their values with respect to the topics under discussion in the group.
    c. Leaders have the ethical responsibility to challenge members to question their values.
    d. Leaders ought to keep their values to themselves lest they sway group members.
    e. _____

27. In which of the following ways do you think you are most likely to influence your group members?

    a. I might encourage them to talk about areas that I deem important.
    b. I'd work at not influencing them.
    c. I'd give them reinforcement if they accepted my beliefs.
    d. I'd pay closer attention to them if they were exploring topics that I deemed relevant.
    e. _____

28. Is it possible for the group leader to keep his or her values out of the group sessions?

    a. Yes, I think it is desirable.
    b. No, I don't think this is either desirable or possible.
    c. I think it would negatively affect the group process.
    d. I see this as basically dishonest.
    e. _____

29. What is your reaction to the guideline that states that leaders should treat each member "equally and individually"?

    a. I think this is a good goal to strive toward.
    b. I do not think it is a reasonable standard.

c. I think that most leaders have favorites, but they should not act upon their feelings of wanting to treat these members in special ways.

d. Leaders can be expected to treat members individually, but not necessarily equally.

e. _____

30. What would you do if you had knowledge of a colleague who rather consistently demonstrated unethical behavior in his or her group work?

a. I would feel an obligation to rectify or disclose incompetencies or unethical behavior.

b. I would begin by confronting the leader with the apparent violation of ethical guidelines.

c. If the colleague did not alter the unethical behavior, I'd report him or her to the chairperson of the ASGW Ethical and Professional Standards Committee.

d. I'd ignore the situation, because most group leaders behave unethically in many situations.

e. _____

3

GROUP LEADERSHIP

PROBLEMS AND ISSUES FACING
BEGINNING GROUP LEADERS

The corresponding chapter in the textbook deals with several common problems that group leaders (both those who are beginning and those who are experienced) typically face. Assume that you are now leading or co-leading a group (even though you may not have done so) and give your reactions to each of the following situations. What do you imagine you'd think and feel in each of these cases? Think about your possible courses of action, then discuss these situations in your class/group and exchange ideas. There are plenty of role-playing activities that can be generated from the material that follows.

1. Imagine yourself getting ready to co-lead your first group. What kind of anxiety would you experience? What would be your main concerns before you actually began the first session? Assume you are meeting your co-leader an hour before the group meets. What things do you think you'd say?

2. Many beginning group leaders are afraid to make mistakes, and out of their fear they may tend to be very inactive and may not try interventions or follow their intuitions. How does this description apply to you? Can you think of some ways that you might challenge yourself and push yourself to be active as a leader? Are you willing to risk making mistakes in doing this? (It would be useful to discuss in small groups the ways in which being afraid of making mistakes might result in passive leading and also ways in which you could become more active.)

3. Again, in small groups, discuss your thoughts on the topic of leader self-disclosure. How do you decide <u>what</u>, <u>when</u>, and <u>how</u> to disclose in

order to make self-disclosure facilitate, rather than interfere with, the group process? Tell others in your group what you are likely to disclose (or not disclose) in a group you are leading, and get their feedback. In your discussion groups, work toward developing a brief list of guidelines for appropriate leader disclosure that you can agree on.

4. I believe that it is extremely important for group counselors to be aware of the personal traits and characteristics needed to become an effective leader. Select some of the following questions to discuss in your class or small group, and use them as a basis for self-reflection on effective leadership.

   a. Why do you want to lead groups?

   b. What do you have to offer as a group counselor?

   c. What experiences have you had that you think will contribute to your success?

   d. What shortcomings do you have that may limit your effectiveness as a leader?

   e. Do you feel a sense of personal power in your own right, or do you depend on a role or position to give you power?

   f. In what ways do you appreciate, value, respect, accept, and like yourself?

   g. Do you see yourself as having courage? In what ways do you see courage as important for a group leader?

SKILLS IN OPENING AND CLOSING GROUP SESSIONS

I've observed that group leaders in training are frequently ineffective in opening and closing group meetings. For example, I've often seen leaders quickly focus on one group member at the beginning of a session with no mention of the previous session. Members should at least be given a brief opportunity to share what they did in the way of practice outside of the group since the last session. Additionally, I find that it is useful to have each member briefly state what he or she wants from the upcoming session. Closing a group session should entail more than an abrupt announcement of the end of the meeting. It's more productive for the group leader to lead everyone in summarizing, integrating, and helping one another find ways of applying what they've learned in the group to outside situations.

The following phrases, statements, and questions will give you some concrete tools that you can use to develop skills in opening and closing group sessions. Review this list frequently, and experiment with parts of it at different times. Add your own opening and closing statements to help you get sessions moving well and end each of your meetings most effectively. I hope you will not employ these phrases mechanically; rather, you should find a way to introduce them in timely and appropriate ways. Eventually, some of these catalytic statements can become a natural part of your own leadership style.

Guidelines for Opening Group Sessions

• What do you want most from today's session?

• Last week we left off with _____.

• Did anyone have any afterthoughts about our last meeting?

• What did you do this week with what you learned in the last session?

• I'd like to go around the group and have each person complete the sentence "Right now I am feeling _____."

• How would each of you like to be different today from the way you were last session?

• Let's go around the group and have each person briefly say what his or her issues or agendas are for this session. What does each of you want from the group today?

• I'd like to share some of my thoughts regarding our last session.

• My expectations and hopes for this session are _____.

• If you did not participate in the group today, how would that be for you?

• Let's all close our eyes. Realize that the next two hours are set aside for you. Ask yourself what you want and what you are willing to do in the group today to get it.

• How is each of you feeling about being here today?

• What are you willing to do to make this session productive?

• Could we have a report on how you are doing with your homework assignments?

• If you are here only because you are required to be, are you still willing to keep yourself open to getting something from the session?

• What would you have to lose if you participated?

• Before we begin, I'd like each of you to sit quietly for a few minutes and do whatever is necessary to bring yourself into the room as fully as possible.

• Today marks the halfway point for our group. We have ten weeks remaining, and I'd like to discuss whether there is anything you'd like to change during the next ten weeks? How would each of you like to be different?

• Do any of you have any issues that you'd like to pursue?

• Is there any unfinished business from the last session that anyone wants to pursue?

- I'd like to go around the group and have each person finish the sentence "Today I could be actively involved in the group by _____."

What other phrases can you add that you think are good leads for opening a group meeting?

_____

_____

_____

_____

_____

_____

Guidelines for Closing Group Sessions

- Before we end for today, is there anything anyone wants to say to anyone else in here?

- What, if anything, did you learn in today's session?

- What did you hear yourself or someone else say that seemed especially significant to you?

- If you were to summarize the key themes that were explored today, what would they be?

- What was it like to you to be here today?

- What would each of you like to do between now and the next session?

- Are there any issues anyone wants to work on at the next session?

- Could we quickly go around the group and have everyone say a few words about how this session was for him or her?

- I'd like to go around the group and have each of you complete the sentence "One thing I need to practice outside of the group is _____."

- Would each of you finish the sentence "The thing I like best (or least) about this session was _____."

- Let's spend the last ten minutes talking about your plans for the coming week. What is each of you willing to do outside of the group?

- A homework assignment I'd like you to consider is _____.

- Does anyone want to give anyone else any feedback?

• Are there any changes you'd like to make in the group?

• How is the group going for you so far?

• How much have you contributed to your group so far?

• We had quite an intense session today. I'm wondering if anyone feels "left hanging" and would like to say how he or she is feeling now.

• Several of you opened up some difficult problems. Although you don't have solutions to those problems, I hope you'll think about the feedback you received.

• Before we close, I'd like to share my own reactions concerning this session.

• I noticed that you were very quiet during the session. Are you willing to say how this meeting was for you?

• You opened up some pretty scary feelings. You made important steps, and I'd like to go ahead in future sessions with what you are discovering.

• Many of you seemed rather lethargic today. I'd like to spend a few minutes before closing to talk about what this might mean.

    List other phrases for closing a meeting.

_____

_____

_____

_____

_____

_____

CHECKLIST AND SELF-EVALUATION OF GROUP-LEADER SKILLS

    The textbook gives a brief but specific list of group-leader skills. The following form will help you review them and provide you with a self-inventory of your strengths as a group leader and specific areas that need improvement. Read the brief description of each skill, and then rate yourself. Next, think about the questions listed under each skill; these will help you determine your level of skill development and examine your behavior as a leader. Ask yourself which skills you most need to develop or improve.
    You can profit from this checklist by reviewing it before and after group sessions. If you are working with a co-leader, it could be very useful to have him or her also rate you on each of these skills. These questions

can also provide a systematic framework for exploring your level of skill development with fellow students and with your supervisor or instructor.

On these 21 skills, rate yourself on a five-point scale, using this code:

5 = I do this most of the time with a very high degree of competence.

4 = I do this much of the time with a high degree of competence.

3 = I do this sometimes with an adequate degree of competence.

2 = I do this occasionally with a relatively low level of competence.

1 = I rarely demonstrate this or do it with an extremely low level of competence.

You are strongly encouraged to take this self-inventory at three points during the semester or quarter. The three blank spaces to the left of each number are for these ratings. I recommend that you cover your previous ratings with a piece of paper so that you are not influenced by them. It is ideal if you rate yourself (and have your co-leader and supervisor rate you) about every five weeks. This will give you a regular pattern of your progress in developing group-leadership skills. Above all, strive for the maximum degree of honesty with yourself as you complete this rating scale and as you reflect on the questions concerning each of these skills.

It is a good idea to circle the letter of the questions that are the most meaningful to you, as well as the questions that indicate a need for further skill development or special attention.

To what degree does the group leader demonstrate the following:

_____ _____ _____   1. Active listening: hearing, understanding, and communicating that one is doing this.
  a. How well do you listen to members?
  b. How attentive are you to nonverbal language?
  c. Are you able to detect incongruity between members' words and their nonverbal cues?
  d. Are you able to hear both direct and subtle messages?
  e. Do you teach members how to listen and to respond?
  f. Do you focus on content to the extent that you miss how a message is delivered?

_____ _____ _____   2. Restating: capturing the essence of what is said in different words with the effect of adding meaning or clarifying meaning.
  a. Can you repeat the essence of what others say without becoming mechanical?
  b. Do your restatements add meaning to what was said by a member?
  c. Do your restatements eliminate ambiguity and give sharper focus to what was said?
  d. Do you check with members to determine if they think your restatement was accurate?

_____ _____ _____ 3. <u>Clarifying</u>: focusing on underlying issues and assisting others to get a clearer picture of what they are thinking or feeling.
   a. Do your clarifying remarks assist members in sorting out conflicting feelings?
   b. Are you able to focus on underlying issues?
   c. Do members get a clearer focus on what they are thinking and feeling?
   d. Does your clarification lead to a deeper level of member self-exploration?

_____ _____ _____ 4. <u>Summarizing</u>: tying together loose ends, identifying common themes, and providing a picture of the directional trends of a group session.
   a. Do you use summarizing as a way to give more direction to a session?
   b. Do you tie together various themes in a group?
   c. Are you able to identify key elements of a session and present them as a summary of the proceedings at the end of a session?

_____ _____ _____ 5. <u>Questioning</u>: using questions to stimulate thought and action and to avoid a question/answer pattern of interaction between leader and member.
   a. Do you avoid overusing questioning as a leadership style?
   b. Do you use open-ended questions to encourage deeper exploration of issues?
   c. Do your questions lead clients in a definite direction? Do you have a hidden agenda? Do you have an expected answer?
   d. Do you model for members a low-level questioning style?
   e. Do you avoid bombarding members with questions that set up a question/answer format?
   f. Do you ask "what" and "how" questions, or "why" questions?
   g. Do you keep yourself hidden as a counselor through questioning, instead of making statements?

_____ _____ _____ 6. <u>Interpretation</u>: explaining the meaning of behavior patterns within the framework of a theoretical system.
   a. Can you present your interpretations in a tentative way as a hunch or a hypothesis?
   b. Are your interpretations dogmatic and authoritarian? Do you have a need to convince members of what you see as "truth"?
   c. Do you have a tendency to rescue members from difficult feelings too quickly through the use of interpretations?
   d. Are you conscious of appropriateness and timing in making interpretations?
   e. Do you encourage members to provide their own meaning of their behavior?

      f. Do you invite other members to make interpretations?

_____ _____ _____ 7. <u>Confrontation</u>: challenging members in a direct way on discrepancies and in such a manner that they will tend to react nondefensively to the confrontation.
      a. <u>How</u> do you confront members? What are the effects of your confrontations, generally?
      b. What kind of model do you provide for confronting others with care and respect?
      c. As a result of your confrontations, are members encouraged to look at discrepancies in a nondefensive manner?
      d. Do you confront people about their unused strengths?
      e. Are you sensitive to the timing and appropriateness of your confrontations?
      f. Are your confrontations related to specific behavior, rather than being judgmental?

_____ _____ _____ 8. <u>Reflecting feelings</u>: mirroring what others appear to be feeling without being mechanical.
      a. Do you reflect feelings accurately?
      b. Do your reflections foster increased contact and involvement?
      c. Do your reflections help members clarify what they are feeling?

_____ _____ _____ 9. <u>Support</u>: offering some form of positive reinforcement at appropriate times in such a way that it has a facilitating effect.
      a. Do you recognize the progress that members make?
      b. Do you build on the strengths and gains made by members?
      c. Do you make use of positive reinforcement and encouragement?
      d. Does your support allow and encourage members to both express and explore their feelings? Or does your support tend to bolster members and aid them in avoiding intense feelings?

_____ _____ _____ 10. <u>Empathy</u>: intuitively sensing the subjective world of others in a group, being able to adopt the frame of reference of others, and communicating this understanding to clients so that they feel understood.
      a. Are your life experiences diverse enough to provide a basis for understanding the subjective world of a range of clients?
      b. Are you able to demonstrate the ability to adopt the internal frame of reference of the client and communicate to that person that you do deeply understand?
      c. Are you able to maintain your separate identity at the same time as you empathize with others?

_____ _____ _____ 11. Facilitating: helping members to clarify their own goals and to take the steps to reach them.
  a. How much do you encourage member interaction?
  b. Do you foster autonomy among the members by assisting them to accept an increasing degree of responsibility for directing their group?
  c. Are you successful in teaching members how to focus on themselves?
  d. Do you foster the spirit in members to identify and express whatever they are feeling as it relates to the here-and-now process of group interaction?

_____ _____ _____ 12. Initiating: demonstrating an active stance in intervening in a group at appropriate times.
  a. Do you have the skills to get group sessions started in an effective manner?
  b. Are you able to initiate new work with others once a given member's work is concluded?
  c. Do you take active steps to prevent the group from floundering in unproductive ways?
  d. Are you able to get interaction going among members or between yourself and members?
  e. Do you avoid initiating to the degree that members assume an active stance?

_____ _____ _____ 13. Goal setting: being able to work cooperatively with members so that there is an alignment between member goals and leader goals, and being able to assist members in establishing concrete goals.
  a. Do you help members establish clear and specific goals?
  b. Are you able to help members clarify their own goals?
  c. Do you encourage members to develop contracts and homework assignments as ways of reaching their goals?
  d. Do you impose your goals on the members without making them partners in the goal-selection process?

_____ _____ _____ 14. Feedback: giving information to members in such a way that they can use it to make constructive behavior changes.
  a. Do you continually give concrete and useful feedback to members, and do you encourage members to do this for one another?
  b. Is your feedback both honest and personal?
  c. Do you teach members to sift through feedback and ultimately decide what they will do with this· information?
  d. Do you offer feedback that relates to both the strengths and weaknesses of members?
  e. How do members typically react when you give them feedback?

34

_____ _____ _____ 15. Suggestion: offering information or possibilities for action that can be used by members in making independent decisions.
   a. Can you differentiate between suggesting and prescribing?
   b. Do you give too many suggestions, and are they just ways of providing quick solutions for every problem a member presents?
   c. Do you rush in too quickly to give advice or information, or do you encourage group members to provide themselves with possible courses of action?
   d. Do you invite others in the group to offer suggestions for members to consider?
   e. Do your directions and suggestions actually restrict members from becoming autonomous?

_____ _____ _____ 16. Protecting: actively intervening to ensure that members will be safeguarded from unnecessary psychological risks.
   a. Do you take measures to safeguard members from unnecessary risks?
   b. Do you show good judgment in risky situations?
   c. Do you intervene when members are being treated unfairly or are being pressured by others?
   d. Do you talk with members about the possible psychological risks involved in group participation?

_____ _____ _____ 17. Self-disclosure: willingly sharing with members any persistent personal reactions that relate to the here-and-now occurrences in the group.
   a. What is your style of self-disclosure? Are you aloof? Do you remain hidden behind a role? Do you model appropriate self-disclosure?
   b. What impact do your self-disclosures tend to have on the group?
   c. Are you willing to reveal your present feelings and thoughts to members when it is appropriate?

_____ _____ _____ 18. Modeling: demonstrating to members desired behaviors that can be practiced both during and between group sessions.
   a. What kind of model are you for your clients?
   b. What specific behaviors and attitudes do you model?
   c. Are you doing in your own life what you ask the members in your group to do?
   d. What might the members of your group know about you by observing your actions in the group?

_____ _____ _____ 19. Use of silence: dealing effectively with silence and the meaning underlying it.
   a. Are you intimidated by silence in the group?
   b. Can you differentiate between useful silences and silences that are a form of resistance?

       c. What do you <u>do</u> with silence? Ignore it? Encourage members to look for its meaning? Use a technique to get action in the group? Ask questions?

       d. Do you tend to intervene quickly to break silences because you are uncomfortable?

_____ _____ _____ 20. <u>Blocking</u>: being able to intervene effectively, without attacking anyone, when members engage in counterproductive behaviors.

       a. Do you take active steps to intervene when there are counterproductive forces within a group?

       b. Do you generally block the following behaviors when you are aware of them: scapegoating? group pressure? questioning? storytelling? gossiping?

       c. Do you block counterproductive behavior in a firm yet sensitive manner?

_____ _____ _____ 21. <u>Terminating</u>: creating a climate that encourages members to continue working after sessions.

       a. Do you attempt to get members to transfer what they are learning in the group to their everyday lives?

       b. Do you assist members in reviewing and integrating their experiences?

       c. Do you create a climate wherein members are encouraged to continue to think and act after sessions?

Suggestions for Using the Checklist

Obviously, all of the preceding 21 items are not merely skills to learn. Many of them represent attitudes related to your leadership effectiveness; some represent personal characteristics that many writers think are ideal qualities of group leaders. Again, you are encouraged to complete this self-evaluation three times during the course and to use it when you actually lead groups.

Finally, I recommend again that you look over the list and circle the numbers of those items that are most important to you. Then use the following guide to summarize your major strengths, the areas you most need to improve, and the areas that you would like to explore more fully in class. Also, it could be valuable to make comparisons of these ratings; for example, how does your self-rating compare with ratings by your supervisor, your co-leader, and the members of your group?

1. Some areas where I feel particularly strong are: _____

_____

_____

_____

_____

2. Areas that need improvement most are: _____

_____

_____

_____

_____

_____

_____

3. Some specific steps I can begin to take now to work toward improving these skills, attitudes, behaviors, and personal characteristics are:

_____

_____

_____

_____

_____

_____

_____

GUIDELINES FOR MEETING WITH YOUR CO-LEADER

In the textbook I make frequent reference to learning to work effectively with a co-leader. If you are working with a co-leader, I cannot overemphasize the value of making the time to meet regularly with him or her before and after group sessions. My students say that, in addition to talking about the progress of members in their group and the progress of the group as a whole, they find it helpful to talk about their relationship with their co-leader. To provide you with some framework for assessing how well you and your co-leader are functioning as a team, I've prepared the following questions. You might look over this list often in your meetings with your co-leader and select those issues that pertain to your relationship at various times. You can identify the areas in which you see yourself functioning especially well and those areas that both of you need to work on improving.

1. Did you select your co-leader, or were the two of you assigned to each other? To what degree is there a trusting relationship between you? Do you respect each other? Are your differences complementary, or do they present problems in your functioning as a therapeutic team?

2. Did the two of you make plans and preparations together as the group was being organized? Are both of you actively involved and interested in the group now?

3. Are you making the time to meet between group sessions on a regular basis? How productive are your meetings? Do you focus exclusively on your group and the members? Or are you also willing to talk about your reactions to the group, to the members, and to each other.

4. Are your theoretical orientations compatible? How do your theoretical views affect the goals and procedures of your group?

5. Do you and your co-leader agree on the division of responsibility between the leaders and the members? Are the two of you sharing leadership responsibility to the satisfaction of each of you?

6. Are the two of you together in your expectations of the group?

7. How are the members reacting to each of you as a leader? How are you and your co-leader reacting to each member? Is either of you having particular difficulty with any member?

8. Do both of you feel free to initiate suggestions and techniques in the group? Is either of you "holding back" and hoping that the other will do most of the leading?

9. Are both of you paying attention to how you open the group sessions and how you bring each session to a close?

10. Does each of you think of ways to continually evaluate the progress of individual members and the group as a whole? Do you have some systematic feedback from the members about how they respond to your leadership?

11. Are you in agreement with your co-leader about self-disclosure? Do both of you reveal to the members your reactions to what is going on in the group? If you see things differently from your co-leader, are you open about this in the group? How do you handle problems between the two of you? Are you competitive with each other? Can you talk openly with the members about your relationship and the way you lead together?

12. What is the balance between confrontation and support in your group? Does one of the team typically support the members and the other challenge them? Are both of you able to be appropriately supportive and confrontive?

13. How do your two styles of leadership blend, and what effect does your co-leadership have on the group?

14. Do both of you spend time talking about how it is for each of you to lead with the other? Are you able to tell your co-leader what you like and do not like about working as a team?

15. Are the two of you reviewing each session and paying attention to any changes in the direction of the group? Can you profit from any mistakes that you have made? What are you learning about yourselves and about groups by co-leading? Are you devoting some time to making plans for upcoming sessions? And are you able to abandon your plans if it is called for in a particular session?

4

EARLY STAGES IN THE DEVELOPMENT OF A GROUP

GUIDELINES FOR WRITING A PROPOSAL FOR A GROUP

A clear and convincing proposal is often essential for translating a good idea for a group into actual practice. If you are going to create a group under the auspices of your supervisors or an agency, you will probably have to explain your rationale and proposed methods. It is useful to write out your proposal, for doing so can help you conceptualize your goals, procedures, and strategies for evaluation.

The following guidelines provide you with some direction in designing a group. To gain practice in developing, writing, and presenting a proposal, think of a group that you'd eventually like to organize. Once you have decided on a particular type of group (for example, a group for parents who want to learn better skills in parenting; or a group for children in an elementary school; or a group for adolescents who are having problems in school), then consider the following questions in drafting your proposal. Later, it would be a good idea to spend some time in class discussing the various members' proposals and getting feedback from others on how to improve your proposal.

1. What type of group will it be? A counseling group? a therapy group? a personal-growth group? a consciousness-raising group? long-term or short-term? Will the group have a remedial (treatment) or a developmental (enhancement) focus?

2. Whom is the group for? For a particular population, such as children in an elementary school? for out-patients in a community mental-health center? for substance abusers in a residential setting? for parents who are having major problems in relating to their children? for couples who hope to learn better communication skills?

3. What are your goals for this group; that is, what will members gain from participating in the group? What are the short-term goals? Are the goals and objectives specific? How will these goals be accomplished in a group setting? How will the long-range goals of the group be evaluated during the course of the group and once the group comes to an end?

4. Why do you believe that there's a need for such a group? In what ways would a group provide definite advantages over individual counseling?

5. What are your basic assumptions underlying this project? Do you have a clear and convincing rationale for your group? Are you able to answer questions that might be raised?

6. Who will lead the group? What are his or her qualifications? If you will be leading the group, will you be doing so alone, or will you be working with a co-leader? What have you learned from doing previous groups that you could apply to the proposed group?

7. What are some of the ways that you will announce your group and recruit members for it? Where will you get members? What will you want to convey in any written announcements?

8. What kind of screening and selection procedures will be used? What is the rationale for using these particular procedures? Whom will you include, and whom might you exclude?

9. How many members will be in the group? Where will the group meet? How often will it meet? How long will each meeting last? Will new people be allowed to join the group once it has started?

10. What kind of structure will the group have? Will the group be designed around special topics and issues? If so, what are some examples of the topics that are likely to be the focus of the group?

11. How will group members be prepared to derive the maximum benefit from the group experience? What are some of the ground rules that will be a basic part of the group?

12. Will you ask members to formulate contracts as a basis for structuring the sessions? What are some advantages and disadvantages of using contracts for your particular group?

13. How will you handle the fact that people will be taking some risks by participating in the group? What will you tell the members about these risks, and what will you do to safeguard members from unnecessary risks? Will you take any special precautions with participants who are minors?

14. Will your group be voluntary or mandatory? If the members are required to attend, what measures are you taking to increase the chances of gaining their cooperation? How might you deal with the resistance of members who do not want to participate?

15. What ethical considerations need to be addressed? Does your proposal reflect an awareness of ethical practice? What ethical guidelines will you follow?

16. What are some examples of techniques and procedures that you might employ in the group? Will there be structured exercises? Will you emphasize role playing? Will members be expected to practice new skills outside of the group sessions? What techniques might you use to get members to support one another in their efforts to change, both in the sessions and between meetings?

17. To what extent will you be available on an individual basis for consultation with group members? If the members are having difficulties resulting from the group, are you willing to meet with them privately, or would you expect them to bring up these problems in the group? When might you suggest a referral for a particular member?

18. What evaluation procedures do you plan? Will you evaluate each session? If so, how? Once the group ends, what methods might you use to assess the overall effectiveness of the group?

19. What follow-up procedures might you use? Will you meet each member privately to discuss the degree to which he or she has met personal goals? Will you meet with the group as a whole one or more times for evaluation purposes?

20. What do you expect to be the characteristics of the various stages of the group? What do you see as your function at each of these stages? What expectations do you have for the members at each of the phases in the development of the group?

EXERCISES AND ACTIVITIES

Your knowledge of the stages in the development of a group can help you carry out the specific functions of a group leader at these various phases. You can provide needed structure, make appropriate interventions, and predict certain blocks to group process. The exercises and activities below will give you practice in your class or group in developing the leadership skills needed at each stage. As you read through these activities, select the ones that have the most meaning for you and bring them up in the class/group. You can use some of them on your own as a way of learning techniques for organizing groups, establishing and maintaining a working climate, terminating groups, and opening or closing group sessions.

1. Imagine talking to potential group members. Explain to them what your group is for and how you expect to lead it. Assume that these people have never been in a group before. What would you stress regarding its purposes and procedures?

2. Screening-interview exercise. Assume the role of a group leader conducting a screening interview for members of a certain kind of group. Conduct a pregroup interview with a prospective member for about ten minutes. Then, the one who was interviewed can report on how he or she felt during the interview. What is your interviewing style like? What were some of the most effective questions or interventions? How could the interview have been improved? Next, interview another prospective member so that you can gain from the feedback and try new ideas.

3. **Group member interviews the leader.** Prospective members may want to talk with the leader before they commit themselves to a group. In this exercise the same format can be used as in Exercise 2, except the <u>group member</u> (several people in class can volunteer for this role) asks questions of the group leader. This exercise can be done in subgroups so that everyone has a chance to be both the group member and the group leader. Everyone can be invited to make observations and suggestions.

4. Draw up a list of specific questions you might ask at a screening interview. What would you look for? On what basis would you include and exclude members?

5. How would you turn away a person if you thought either that he or she was not appropriate for the group or that the group was not appropriate for him or her? You might set this up as a group/class exercise. Are you able to not accept a person in a group without conveying rejection?

6. What screening methods, if any, could you apply to an involuntary population? Do you believe that people who are involuntarily in a group can benefit from it? Why or why not? How would you deal with the situation if the agency you worked for insisted that all of the clients attend the group, whether they wanted to or not? Assume that all the mental-health workers there had to use group therapy as the primary treatment method.

7. What would be your rationale for deciding on a homogeneous or a heterogeneous group? Discuss your reasons for your preference. What characteristics would you want group members to have in common?

8. Discuss some of the problems that you might encounter in an open group that you would not be so likely to have in a closed group. How do you expect to deal with the problems that arise in an open group (one with changing membership)?

9. What value, if any, do you see in arranging an initial private interview with each group member to explore matters such as goals, fears, expectations, questions, and concerns? How would you prepare members of your group?

10. <u>Initial stages of a group.</u> Try to recall what it was like for you when you first entered a counseling group <u>or</u> any group of strangers. Consider the possibility that your prospective group members feel the same way. Discuss with others in your class/group how you might be a more compassionate leader if you could keep these memories fresh.

11. <u>Initial-session exercise.</u> To give you practice in opening a new group, form subgroups of about eight people. Two of you can volunteer to be co-leaders, and the rest are members. The co-leaders' task is to give a brief orientation. Consider some of the following ideas for orienting your group:

    a. Give about a ten-minute <u>preparation talk</u> to group members. Tell them the things you'd <u>most</u> want them to know so that they could function more effectively as participants throughout the course of the group.

b. Consider discussing the purpose of the group, the nature of the group as you see it, any ground rules, and any other pertinent information.

c. Think about telling the members something about yourself. Why are you leading groups? How do you get yourself ready for each group session?

The members can be given the opportunity to ask questions or to talk about their expectations. After about half an hour or so, discuss the exercise. Members can share how they felt during the session, and constructive feedback can be given to the co-leaders.

12. Trust building. What do you think are the most crucial tasks during the early stages of a group? Think of the ways that, as a group leader, you would attempt to create trust within the group. Also, think about ways you would introduce yourself to your group and how you'd take care of introductions of group members. What are some specific ways in which you might work on building trust at the initial meetings?

13. What are some possible explanations for the negative feelings and con- flict that typically occur in a group's initial developmental stages, before members feel free enough to experience positive feelings?

14. Most writers describe conflict, confrontations, competition, rivalry, and jockeying for power as a basic part of a group's evolution. What could you do as a leader to ignore these dynamics? What effect would this have on subsequent group development?

15. Assume that you are leading your first group, and several members are questioning your level of expertise. How would you deal with this?

16. Imagine you are a group leader, and the group members are challenging you by telling you that they see you strictly as "the leader." They ask you to become more like they are and share more of yourself with them. How would you handle this situation? Explain to the group your under- standing of the role of group leader.

17. Read the section in the textbook on resistance and forms of avoidance behavior in group members. Examine your own patterns of resistance as a group member. List some ways that you've found yourself resistant in this class/group. How many of the resistant and problem behaviors that are described in the text have you recognized in yourself? Imagine that you are leading a group of people who have many of the same de- fenses and resistances that you have. How would this be for you?

18. In your own experience as a group member, what has helped you to recog- nize and to work through certain resistances? What has hindered you? What might have led you to deeper entrenchment into certain resistances and defensive styles of behaving in a group?

19. Can you respect resistance? Assume that a member says that she doesn't want to press onward with an issue she's been working on. What courses of action would you be inclined to take? Do you see a difference be- tween pressuring members to talk about a given issue and encouraging

them to talk about possible fears that keep them from working on the issue?

20. What can a group leader do in general to effectively handle resistances that occur in a group? What are helpful leader behaviors in a group whose members exhibit problem behaviors?

21. Discuss the differences between reducing a person to a label (such as the monopolist, the help-rejecting complainer, the bore, and so on) and describing a specific behavior such as monopolizing. As a group leader, how can you encourage a member to recognize and deal with specific behaviors that are counterproductive to the progress of both the individual and the group?

22. There is a danger of pushing people too soon to give up a defense. Ask yourself if you are able to handle the reaction of a person who relinquishes a defense. For example, if you encourage a member to feel his anger instead of intellectualizing it, could you handle the possible explosive expression of his rage should he experience it fully? How can you determine whether you are competent to deal with what lies under a defense?

23. Look over the list of "difficult group members" in the textbook. What problem behaviors or difficult members do you anticipate having the most difficulty with? Why? How might you typically respond?

24. One way to help the discussion of dealing with difficult group members come alive is to role-play certain members as you experience them. As a suggestion, you might role-play those behaviors that you find yourself having the most difficulty with as a group leader. Other students in your small group can try out various ways of dealing with the problem behaviors you bring forth. Exercises 25-34 all lend themselves to role playing and discussion. I suggest that you focus on your feelings in these exercises in order to see what you can learn about yourself as you work with different types of resistances and problem behaviors that are typically manifested in groups.

25. Intellectualizing. Assume that a person in the group you're leading talks about herself in a detached manner without emotion. How can you get her to express more affect? How can you help her to realize that she is intellectualizing?

26. Questioning. Monitor yourself as you lead a group. To what degree do you rely on questioning as a style in your group leading? Are you modeling a question/answer style for members? Consider telling people what you want from them instead of questioning them. What might happen if you first gave your reasons for asking a question and then proceeded to ask your question?

27. Advice-giving. Assume that a particular member continually gives advice every time a member talks about a struggle. How might you deal with such a member who typically tells others what they should do?

28. Support versus Band-Aiding.

    a. Imagine yourself explaining to a group the difference between genuine support and Band-Aiding. What would you tell them?

    b. Assume that a member gives support to everyone in the group yet does not seem to be able to ask for support or handle it when it is directed toward her. What might you say to her?

    c. Now assume that you confront a person who interrupts and attempts to make others feel positive whenever they experience any discomfort or pain. The person snaps back: "I'm just trying to help. Why do you like to see people suffer"? How would you explain your rationale for implying that this person's support at that moment was not useful?

29. Avoidance. A member in a group you're leading not only avoids sharing himself in the group but is also successful in sidetracking what could be productive work of other members. How might you feel toward this kind of person? How would you deal with him?

30. Dealing with silent members.

    a. How can you determine the difference between silence that is productive and silence that is a defense?

    b. Assume you have a silent member, one who rarely speaks even if she is encouraged to do so. What do you think would be the effects of the following strategies?

        • Call on her.

        • Ignore her.

        • Ask the group members how they feel about her being silent.

        • Tell her that you are aware of her silence and that you are interested in what she has to say.

        • Pay close attention to her nonverbal messages.

        • Remind her of her contract to be a participant.

        • Ask her what is stopping her from speaking.

        • Ask her if her silence is satisfactory to her.

    What other approaches would you consider?

    c. How would you respond to a member who says: "I learn a lot by listening. I'm the type who observes. I've never been much of a talker, but I do get something from listening to what others have to say."

31. Monopolizing. How would you respond to a person who dominated the group you were leading? What are some ways that you can think of to effectively work with a member who exhibits a great need for continual attention and whose attention-getting behavior disrupts the group?

32. <u>Storytelling</u>. Assume that you confront a person who is storytelling. He responds by saying: "I'm hurt and confused. I felt I was risking a lot by telling you all about a private matter, and now you tell me that I'm storytelling. This makes me want to pull back and not say anything." What would you reply to him? What can you say about the difference between facilitative self-disclosure and pseudo-self-disclosure?

33. <u>Dependency</u>.

   a. How would you respond to these forms of dependency?

   - the person who makes no move without consulting with you

   - the person who seeks continual reassurance from everyone in the group

   - the person who appears to listen and then proceeds to tell you why what you said won't work

   - the person who claims that he'd be utterly lost without this weekly group

   b. What might <u>you</u> as a group leader get from the dependency of clients on you? Which of your needs might foster their dependency?

34. <u>Hostile-aggressive behavior</u>. What would you do if you had an extremely hostile member (one who was indirect with his anger), whose effect on the group was to close others up? Explain your course of action.

35. In my experience in consulting and doing in-service workshops with people who lead groups, I've found that there is a tendency to focus on group members' behavior problems as a justification for the group's lack of success. What suggestions do you have that will enable you to focus on your own feelings and reactions? How can you avoid the pitfall of blaming "problem clients" for difficulties in a group, while leaving your own dynamics out of this process? How might you use members' problem behaviors to avoid your own responsibility? How might you creatively find avenues for expressing your own feelings and reactions toward problem behaviors you encounter in a group?

36. As you lead groups, some members may develop transference toward you. This can consist of both positive and negative reactions to you, yet in many senses transference comprises feelings that members have or had toward significant people in their lives. Consider how you'd feel, what you'd think, how you'd respond, and what you might do as certain participants developed unrealistic views of you by casting you into each of the following fixed roles that met their needs:

   a. You are seen and treated as "the expert" and are constantly asked for advice.

   b. You are cast into the role of "authority figure." Certain members consistently feel either that you are judging them or that you are in some way exerting power over them.

   c. Some members see you as the "fully together person." They see you as being without any struggles.

d. Certain members want you for a friend. They seek special attention from you and actively try to develop a friendship that extends beyond the group.

e. You are seen as a potential lover, and you are the recipient of sexually seductive behaviors.

37. Your own objectivity can become distorted as a result of countertransference—feelings that are aroused in you toward certain clients and that tend to be based on unrecognized and unresolved personal issues. Put yourself into each of the following eight common countertransference situations. How would you fit into each of these situations? What are you aware of in yourself that might prevent you from focusing on the needs and best interests of group members?

a. You have an inordinate need for reassurance and constant reinforcement; this includes the need to please all the members, to win their respect, to get them to approve you, and to have them confirm you as a "superb leader."

b. You see yourself in certain clients; you overidentify with some members to the extent that you take on their problems.

c. You develop sexual and romantic feelings toward certain members; you engage in seductive behavior and allow your sexual attraction to become a central focus in the group.

d. You give people advice in such a way that you tell others what to do based on your own needs and values.

e. You develop social relationships with some members outside of the group and find that you challenge them less during group sessions than you do other members.

f. You use power over members to prove your adequacy; you gain power through the use of certain highly directive techniques.

g. You attempt to persuade members to accept the values you hold; you are more interested in having members subscribe to your idea of the right way to live than in letting members decide on their own values.

h. You see clearly the faults of members and use what they do or don't do to justify poor results in a group; at the same time you are blind to your own shortcomings or your part in the group process.

HELPFUL INTERVENTION PHRASES FOR THE
INITIAL STAGE OF A GROUP

A few well-chosen and well-timed words can give group members the guidance that will enable them to explore personal issues in a significant way. Based on my own work with groups and my training of and consultation with group leaders, I have compiled a list of sentences and phrases that leaders can use during the early stage of a group. It might be helpful for you to review the list frequently before you begin a group.

- Are you here because you want to be?

- What do you most want to get from this group?

- What are you willing to do to get what you say you want?

- Are you willing to try out new things in here?

- What are three things you want us to know about you?

- If you were to introduce yourself as the person you'd like to be, what would you tell us about you?

- What do you know about groups? With what expectations are you coming to this group?

- If a friend of yours were to introduce you to this group, what might he or she say about you?

- What was going on in your life that led you to join this group?

- What is it like for you to be here now?

- What fears or doubts do you have about this group, if any?

- What do you imagine would happen if you were to say the most difficult thing?

- What do you fear most? What do you hope for most?

- Why would you want to change anything in your life now?

- What would you most like to say you've learned or decided when you leave the group?

- Realize that you'll take from this group what you are willing to put into it.

- If you are feeling something in here persistently, express it.

- How do you usually introduce yourself? What do you tell people about yourself?

HELPFUL INTERVENTION PHRASES FOR
THE TRANSITION STAGE OF A GROUP

- I've noticed that you have been very quiet during many of these sessions, and I'd like to know how you feel.

- The silence in this group doesn't feel good to me. I wonder what is not being said in here that needs to be expressed?

- Are you willing to continue now?

48

- Imagine that this is the last chance you have to change your life.

- I'd like to check out with the people in here where we are going as a group.

- Are you willing to explore the reasons for your reluctance to pursue this topic further?

- Perhaps you'd be willing to tell us some of the ways in which the situation in this group seems like situations you find yourself in outside the group.

- How are you the same both in the group and in daily life?

- I am having a difficult time with all of the questioning that is going on in here.

- Many of you are quick to give advice, and I want to let you know that I am uncomfortable with this style of interacting.

- Whom do you have unfinished business with in here?

- Are you willing to convert your question into a statement?

- If this were the end of the group, would that be all right?

- I suspect that some of you expect change to be easy, and I sense some of you looking at me for solutions.

- What's the worst thing that you can imagine happening if you continue now?

- If you never change in this respect, would that be so bad?

- What are you willing to do with the tension you feel?

- I'm aware of a good bit of resistance and holding back with many of you in here, and I'd like to talk about this.

- I feel as though I'm working too hard at leading—almost as though I'm pulling teeth. I'd like to check out how others are feeling about this.

- So, some of you say you're bored. What are you willing to do about changing this?

5

LATER STAGES IN THE
DEVELOPMENT OF A GROUP

QUESTIONS FOR DISCUSSION

1. What are the characteristics that distinguish a group in the working stage from a group that is in transition?

2. How is group cohesion a central variable at the working stage? What factors contribute to this cohesion? If a group you were leading seemed fragmented and lacked any sense of community, what might you say or do? Can you think of some reasons to explain the absence of cohesion?

3. In the chapter, review the therapeutic factors of a group. What are a few of these factors that you think are especially important?

4. Refer to the section of the textbook that deals with the characteristics of an effective working group. What factors do you think are most significant? Discuss your reasons.

5. How would you explain to a group member the nature and purpose of self-disclosure? What are some specific guidelines that are useful in teaching participants the skills involved in appropriate self-disclosure?

6. What is the purpose of confrontation? How can it be done by members in a constructive way? What would you tell members about the manner of constructive confrontation?

SELF-ASSESSMENT SCALE:
WHAT KIND OF GROUP MEMBER AM I?

I believe that one of the best ways of preparing for effective group leadership is to first become an effective group member. The following self-inventory is geared to help you determine your strengths and weaknesses as a member. I hope you have already had some form of experience as a member of a group. If not, you can rate yourself on the inventory in terms of your behavior in the class you're now in.

After this inventory is completed, the class can break up into small groups; the groups can be composed of people who know one another best. Members of these groups should then assess the self-ratings and discuss how to become a better group member.

Rate yourself on a scale of 1 to 5, with 1 being "almost never true of me" and 5 being "almost always true of me" as a group member.

_____ 1.   I am an active and contributing group member.

_____ 2.   I am willing to raise personal concerns and explore them in the group.

_____ 3.   I listen attentively to others, and I respond to them.

_____ 4.   I share my perceptions of other members, telling them how I see them and how I am affected by them.

_____ 5.   I confront others with care, yet I do so directly.

_____ 6.   As a group participant, I not only give direct feedback to others but I am also open to considering feedback from them.

_____ 7.   I'm willing to formulate specific goals and contracts when I am a member of a group.

_____ 8.   I'm willing to openly express my feelings about and reactions to what is occurring within the group.

_____ 9.   I serve as a positive model to others in the group.

_____ 10.   I am active in taking steps to create and maintain trust in the group.

_____ 11.   I show that I am willing to put insights into action by practicing what I learn in the group in my life between sessions.

_____ 12.   I prepare myself for the group by thinking about what I want from the sessions.

_____ 13.   I am willing to get involved in role-playing activities.

_____ 14.   I'm able to provide support to others in the group at appropriate times.

GROUP MEMBER'S WEEKLY EVALUATION OF GROUP

Directions: The following evaluation sheet can be given at the end of each group session you may be leading. Using such a device will give you a quick index of the level of satisfaction of the members. You can summarize the results and begin a session with the trends that you are noticing from the evaluation sheets.

Have the members circle the appropriate number for each item, using the following scale:

1 or 2 = very weak

3 or 4 = moderately weak

5 or 6 = adequate

7 or 8 = moderately strong

9 or 10 = very strong

1. What degree of preparation (reacting, thinking about the topic, reading, and writing) did you do for this week?

    1 2   3 4   5 6   7 8   9 10

2. How would you rate your involvement in the group today?

    1 2   3 4   5 6   7 8   9 10

3. How would you rate the group's level of involvement?

    1 2   3 4   5 6   7 8   9 10

4. Rate yourself on the degree to which you saw yourself as willing today to take risks, to share with other members what you thought and felt, and to be an active participant.

    1 2   3 4   5 6   7 8   9 10

5. To what degree do you feel satisfied with your experience in the group?

    1 2   3 4   5 6   7 8   9 10

6. To what degree do you feel that the group dealt with issues in a personal and meaningful way (sharing feelings as opposed to intellectual discussion)?

    1 2   3 4   5 6   7 8   9 10

7. To what degree do you experience trust within the group?

    1 2   3 4   5 6   7 8   9 10

8. How would you rate the group leader's level of involvement and investment in today's session?

    1 2   3 4   5 6   7 8   9 10

9. Rate your leader on the dimensions of his or her ability today to create a good working climate, as characterized by warmth, respect, support, empathy, and trust.

1   2   3 4   5 6   7 8   9 10

A new behavior I tried was: _____

_____

What I would like to do differently at the next meeting is: _____

_____

HELPFUL INTERVENTION PHRASES FOR THE WORKING STAGE OF A GROUP

You might find the following sentences and phrases helpful once your group gets under way and people are working. Again, these are not merely clichés; rather, they are specific statements that can serve as constructive interventions _if_ you use them in context, with a sense for timing. For example, if you sense that a member is leaving something out, you might intervene with "What are you not saying that needs to be said now?" If these brief interventions are done appropriately, members can be given a gentle impetus to continue. As you lead groups, think of the phrases that are useful to you. Below are some that my co-leaders and I use.

- What would you like to do?

- Have any of you had any thoughts about our last session that you'd like to share?

- What else needs to be said?

- How were you affected by _____?

- How does this issue relate to you?

- I'd like each person in the group to finish the sentence "_____ . . ."

- Imagine this is the last chance you have to change your life.

- I'd like you to hold onto this feeling for a little longer.

- Could we have everyone say what he or she is feeling or thinking right now?

- I like it when you _____.

- Right now I am aware of _____.

- Would you be willing to try this experiment to see how it works for you?

- What is your objection to continuing?

- Imagine that the significant person were here now. What would you want to say to her?

- Don't ask him questions. Tell him how it is for you.

- I notice that _____.

- I'm interested in _____.

- I hope you'll consider _____.

- My hunch is _____.

- If your eyes could speak now, what would they say?

- What will help you to remember what is being said to you?

- You experienced a lot of emotions during this session. What did you learn about yourself from this?

- What decision did you make about yourself in that situation when you were a child?

- You may have told yourself as a child that you had to be that way to survive, but now that decision doesn't seem appropriate.

- Become each part of your dream. Give each part a voice.

- Instead of talking about this situation, live it as though it were happening now.

- If your mother were here, what would you say to her now that you didn't tell her then?

- You have continued indoctrinating yourself with propaganda that you got from your parents. What new sentences could you begin to tell yourself?

- Instead of saying "I can't," say "I won't."

- What can you do between this session and the next to practice what you've just learned?

- I think it's important that each of you ask if you are getting what you want from this group and if there are any changes you'd like to see.

- I'd like to review our contracts to determine if any of them need to be revised or updated.

HELPFUL INTERVENTION PHRASES FOR
THE ENDING STAGE OF A GROUP

During the consolidation stage of a group it is important for members to think of ways to apply what they've learned in the group to everyday life,

54

to be able to take care of unfinished business, to be able to express their feelings regarding separation, and to make sense of the total group experience. Some of the following phrases and sentences are ones that I frequently use during the ending stages of a group. As you review this list, think of additional statements and questions that would help members accomplish the tasks at this stage of the group.

- What has this group meant to you?

- What are some of the most important things you have learned about yourself?

- Are there any things you want to say to anyone in here?

- How do you feel about saying good-bye?

- I'm aware of the tendency to forget what we learn in a group, so I'd like to talk about ways that you can remember what you have learned.

- How can you practice what you've learned here?

- How do you think you'll be different? Don't tell them, show them!

- Whom do you need to talk with outside of the group? What is the essence of what you want them to hear?

- What decisions have you made?

- If we were to meet one year from now as a group, what would you want to say that you had accomplished?

- If you had to say your message in one sentence, what would it be?

- Where can you go from here, now that the group is ending?

- How might you discount what you've learned in here?

- How can you translate insight into action?

- I hope each of you will find at least one person in this group to contact if you discover that you aren't putting your plans into action.

- I'd like to spend some time exploring where each of you can go from here, now that our group is ending.

- Let's practice and role-play some of the situations that each of you expects to encounter after you leave the group.

- To what degree did you attain your goals?

- What did it take, and what steps did you go through to get what you wanted out of this group?

- If you are less than satisfied with the outcomes of this group, what did you learn about your role in the group?

- If you could repeat this experience, what might you do differently?

- What kept you from becoming closer to others in this group?

- What did you learn about yourself in this group? And what did you do to bring this learning about?

- What do you most want to take from this group and apply to your everyday life?

PART TWO

Theoretical Approaches to Group Counseling

6

THE PSYCHOANALYTIC APPROACH

PRECHAPTER PRIMERS AND SELF-INVENTORIES—GENERAL DIRECTIONS

The purpose of the primers and self-inventories is to identify and clarify your attitudes and beliefs about the different theoretical approaches to group therapy. Each of the statements on these inventories is <u>true</u> from the perspective of the particular theory in question. You decide the degree to which you agree/disagree with these statements. Complete each self-inventory <u>before</u> you read the corresponding textbook chapter. Respond to each statement, giving the initial response that most clearly identifies how you think or feel. Then, after reading the chapter, look over your responses to see if you want to modify them in any way. These self-inventories will help you express your views and will prepare you to actively read and think about the ideas you'll encounter in each of the chapters on theory.

I suggest that you go over your completed inventories and mark those items you would like to discuss; then bring your inventories to class, and compare your positions with the views of others. Such comparisons can stimulate debate and help get the class involved in the topics to be discussed.

Using the following code, write next to each statement, the number of the response that most closely reflects your viewpoint:

5 = I <u>strongly agree</u> with this statement.

4 = I <u>agree</u>, in most respects, with this statement.

3 = I am <u>undecided</u> in my opinion about this statement.

2 = I <u>disagree</u>, in most respects, with this statement.

1 = I <u>strongly disagree</u> with this statement.

PRECHAPTER PRIMER AND SELF-INVENTORY FOR THE
PSYCHOANALYTIC APPROACH

_____ 1. The key to understanding human behavior is understanding the unconscious.

_____ 2. In group work it is particularly important to focus on experiences from the first five years of life, because the roots of present conflicts usually lie there.

_____ 3. Group work should encourage participants to relive significant relationships, and the group should become a symbolic family so that members can work through these early relationships.

_____ 4. Insight, understanding, and working through repressed material should be given primary focus in group therapy.

_____ 5. Free association, dream work, analysis, and interpretation are essential components of effective group work.

_____ 6. Transference should be encouraged in a group, because it is through this process that members come to an understanding of unresolved conflicts in certain relationships.

_____ 7. Because of the reconstructive element of analytic group work, the process should be a long-term one.

_____ 8. An understanding of the forms resistance takes is essential for the group leader.

_____ 9. Group leaders must be continuously aware of ways that their own feelings (countertransference) can affect the group.

_____ 10. Effective therapy cannot occur unless the causes of a client's problems are identified.

SUMMARY OF BASIC ASSUMPTIONS AND KEY CONCEPTS
OF THE PSYCHOANALYTIC APPROACH

1. The human personality is basically determined by unconscious motivations, irrational forces, sexual and aggressive impulses, and early childhood experiences. Understanding the unconscious is the key to understanding human behavior.

2. Normal personality development is based on a successful resolution of conflicts at various stages of psychosexual development.

3. Psychoanalytic therapists pay particular attention to the unconscious and the early developmental years as crucial determinants of personality and behavior.

4. Because it is necessary for clients to relive and reconstruct their past and work through repressed conflicts in order to understand how the un-

STAGES OF DEVELOPMENT OF THE PSYCHOANALYTIC GROUP*

Dimension	Initial Stage	Working Stage	Final Stage
Key developmental tasks and goals	Key task is uncovering and exploring unconscious material. Focus is on historical causes of present behavior. Unconscious processes are made conscious by promoting freedom to express any thought, fantasy, and feeling.	The group resembles the original family, allowing members to relive their childhood and get to the roots of their conflicts. Key tasks include recalling of early childhood experiences and reworking of past traumas. The basic work entails recognizing and working through resistances and transferences. Multiple transferences occur in the group; members become aware of past relationships that are brought into the present situation in the group.	Key task is the development of insight into causes of problems. Analysis and interpretation of transference continues. Focus is on the conscious personal action that members can take and on social integration. Main goals are for members to analyze and resolve their own transferences and avoid countertransferences toward other members, and to work through the repetition of behavior from early years.
Role of group leader and tasks	Leader offers support and creates a permissive and nonstructured climate. Leader's tasks include setting limits, interpreting, and getting a sense of the members' character structures and patterns of defense.	Leader makes timely interpretations that lead to insight; helps members deal with anxiety constructively; is aware of countertransference; and helps members deal effectively with resistances and transferences in the group.	Leader relinquishes much of the leadership functions to allow the members a greater degree of independence; guides the members to fuller awareness and social integration.
Role of group members	Members build rapport by reporting dreams and fantasies. They are expected to free-associate with one another's dreams. They are expected to work through resistances that prevent unconscious material from becoming conscious.	Members produce material in a free-floating manner; they ventilate and express feelings over past traumas. Emphasis is on working through transferences with leader and members. Members function as adjunct therapists by saying whatever comes to their mind; they also make interpretations for others.	Resistances and transferences are worked through, and focus is on self-interpretation and on reality testing. Members become able to spot their own transference figures and relationships; they also contribute to the interpretation of the transference of others.

*The transition stage has been omitted because there are no clear demarcations between these stages. The intent of these tables is to give readers an idea of early, middle, and ending stages of group.

Techniques		
Individual sessions are used to create readiness for a group. "Go-around" technique is used as a free-association device, where members respond spontaneously to one another. Initial resistances are dealt with.	Main techniques that are used include free association, interpretation, analysis of resistance and transference, interpretation and analysis of dreams, use of alternate sessions, and use of pregroup and postgroup sessions.	Alternate sessions and the pregroup meeting or postgroup meeting may continue. Attempts are made to help members integrate what they've learned in the group.

Questions to consider

At the first group meeting, how can resistances to joining the group best be dealt with?

What are some ways that you can use here-and-now material in the group to understand a member's past? How can one's past provide a framework for understanding current behavior?

What are some values of simply reporting and sharing dreams in a group?

What are some ways to encourage members to give unrehearsed reactions to one another?

How can free association be promoted by the "go-around" technique?

Are members looking to the leader for direction and cues?

How are members relating to others in the group in ways that are similar to how they were in their original family?

How can the group be formed so that the recalling of early childhood experiences can best be worked with?

What are some advantages and disadvantages of the leader's encouraging transference? How can this transference toward the leader be worked with in a therapeutic way?

As a leader, how can you utilize the projections of group members? What techniques can you develop to work with projections?

What are some ways that you can make interpretations of individuals in a group without promoting their dependency on you? How can your interpretations stimulate their searching?

During the final stage, how can members be encouraged to take action based on their insight?

What are some ways of helping members to understand and resolve their transferences to the leader and others in the group?

What are some ways of letting go of the leadership of the group so that the members are encouraged to become increasingly independent?

What are some signs that a member is ready to terminate a group?

How can alternate sessions promote a degree of independence in the members?

What are some dangers of continuing the group for an indefinite period of time? What are the values of long-term group therapy?

How can termination best take place in an analytic group?

Reactions: Summarize your reactions to the psychoanalytic perspective of group developmental stages. What do you like most? least? What aspects of this approach would you incorporate in your style of leadership?

conscious affects one now, psychoanalytic group therapy is intensive and generally involves a long-term commitment.

5. A major portion of group work consists of dealing with resistance, working through transference, experiencing catharsis, developing insight and self-understanding, and learning the relationship between past experiences and their effect on current development.

6. Analytically oriented group practitioners tend to remain relatively anonymous and encourage group members to project onto them the feelings that they have had toward the significant people in their lives. The analysis and interpretation of transference leads to insight and personality change. (Some analytically oriented therapists do not always remain anonymous, however; they may respond to members in personal ways.)

7. Some of the unique advantages of analytic-group-therapy are: members are able to experience relationships that are similar to their own family relationships and thus reexperience some of those early relationships; there are opportunities for multiple transferences; members can gain insight into their defenses and resistances more dramatically than they can in individual therapy; and dependency on the authority of the therapist is lessened, for members get feedback from other members.

EXERCISES AND ACTIVITIES FOR THE PSYCHOANALYTIC APPROACH

Rationale

In this workbook I present a wide range of exercises that are based on particular therapeutic models. Let me emphasize that strict practitioners of each approach may disagree that these exercises present commonly used techniques. My aim is to use the concepts of each therapeutic model to build exercises that you can practice, modify, and adapt to fit your needs. I hope you will develop your own techniques for use in your own group work.

For the exercises in this section I've selected several group techniques that are based on conventional psychoanalytic concepts and procedures and modified them considerably in the hope that you will be able to apply some of them in your group work. The following exercises are geared to stimulate your thinking on issues such as the value of working with the past, being open to what you can learn from the unconscious, experimenting with techniques like free association and dream work, and increasing your appreciation of the importance of central concepts such as resistance, transference, and countertransference. In my opinion, regardless of their theoretical orientation, group practitioners must understand these concepts. As you work through these exercises in your class/group, remain open to ways you can incorporate some of them in your style of leading groups.

Exercises

1. The alternate session. It is a common practice for psychoanalytic groups that meet on a weekly basis with a leader to supplement their sessions with meetings without a formal leader. (Refer to the textbook for a discussion of the rationale of leaderless meetings on a regular basis.) If

you are in a group (as a part of the experience for this course) that meets with a leader, consider having some meetings where the leadership could be shifted among the members. For example, two of you could co-lead the group using the therapeutic model that you are studying that week. Discuss the values and the problems of self-directed or leader-less groups.

2. <u>Working with your past</u>. The analytic approach is based on the assumption that past experiences play a vital role in shaping one's current personality. The following short exercises/questions are designed to assist you in remembering and exploring in your group selected dimensions of your past.

   a. Recall and reconstruct some childhood experiences. Examining pictures of yourself as a child, interviewing people who knew you well, looking over diaries, and so on can be useful means of stimulating recall. Share in your group some of what you consider to be the most significant influences from your past. How have these factors contributed to the person you are now?

   b. Write an outline (such as you might find in the table of contents) of a book that you could write about your life. Pay attention mainly to chapter headings. Examples might include: "The child who was never allowed to be a child"; "A time of abandonment"; "My most joyous memories"; "Dreams I had as a child"; "The things I wanted to be as a child." You could also write the Preface to this book about your life and include an acknowledgment section. Who are the people you'd most want to acknowledge as having a significant impact on your life? In what ways have they made a difference?

   c. In the outline for the book on your life, include a chapter in which you rewrite your past the way you would have wanted it to be. Share your ideas for this chapter with your group.

   d. Make a list of your current struggles, and see if you can trace the origins of these conflicts to childhood events.

   e. Freud believed that the events of the first five years of life are crucial determinants of our personality. What can you find out about this time in your life? What hunches do you have about the effect of your early years on the person you now are?

3. <u>Free association</u>. A key method of unlocking the unconsicous is free association; the therapist asks clients to clear their mind of day-to-day thoughts and simply report in a spontaneous way whatever comes to mind. This "flowing" with feelings and associations can tap underlying unconscious material. When clients block and censor what they are saying, this is seen as resistance to getting into contact with the unconscious. There are several ways to use free association in a group:

   a. For example, members can be encouraged to say whatever comes to them, regardless of how appropriate or meaningful it may seem. Participants often censor their contributions; they rehearse what they will say for fear that "it won't come out right." Some members agonize over what to bring up in a group and exactly how to present a personal issue.

   b. Participants can also be asked to go around to the other group members and say the first thing that they think as they face each person.

During a free-association process, group leaders might identify repressed and blocked material. The sequence of associations gives leaders cues to anxiety-arousing material, and they can begin making connections and then interpreting the meaning of these associations to the client.

c. It might also be a productive exercise in your group to make up incomplete sentences, finish them, and then find ways to free-associate with what seems to be significant material. For example, you might work with sentences such as:

- When I'm in this group I feel _____.

- One way I attempt to avoid things in this group is by _____.

- One fear I have is _____.

- One way I isolate myself at times is by _____.

4. Dream work. Report the key elements of one of your dreams to your group. You might try the following suggestions as a way of learning something about yourself through your dreams.

a. Select any part of your dream and free-associate with that part. Say as many words as fast as you can without censoring them. After you've done this, see what your free-association work tells you.

b. Give an initial interpretation of your dream. What themes or patterns do you see?

c. Next, ask group members to give their interpretations of your dream. What do they think your dream means?

d. If they want to, other group members can free-associate with any parts of your dream.

You might want to begin keeping a dream journal. Write down your dreams. Record what you remember. Then look at the patterns of your dreams and interpret their meaning.

5. Resistance. Brainstorm all the possible ways in which you might resist in a group. What resistances have you experienced to simply getting into a group? List some avoidance patterns that you have seen in yourself in a group. Next, discuss some possible causes of resistance in group members. What might they be defending themselves against? What are some ways that you can think of to help group members recognize and work through resistances that could prevent them from effectively working in a group? What are some uses of resistances? What purposes do these member resistances serve?

6. Transference. A central concept in analytic-group therapy is the identification and working through of transference. To get some idea of this process, try some of these exercises in your group.

a. Go around to each person in the group. Does anyone remind you of a significant person in your life? Discuss the similarities. (Select people who have caused especially strong reactions in you.)

b. You can also explore possible transferences that occur outside of the group. Have you ever experienced strong, immediate, and even irrational reactions to a person you hardly knew? Discuss what you can learn about unfinished business from your past by focusing on such occurrences.

c. Be aware of transference onto the leader as an authority figure. Discuss the ways in which you might work with this therapeutically. How might such transferences block growth?

7. Countertransference.

   a. What kind of client do you think you'd have the most difficulty working with in a group? Why? How do you imagine that you'd handle a client who had very strong negative feelings toward you, especially if you felt that these feelings were inappropriate and a function of transference? How might you handle a group member with the same degree of intense feelings (also transference) if they were positive ones? What personal needs or unresolved conflicts within you could make it difficult for you to work with members with either positive or negative transference?

   b. Select a client who you think is a difficult group member and who you anticipate will cause you problems. Become this client. Take on this person's characteristics as fully as you can. Others in the group can function as members, and one person can be the group leader and attempt to work with you. (Several members might want to get some experience being the leader and working with you, each using a different approach.) After you've had a chance to take on the role of this "problem member" for a while, explore what this experience was like for you. How did the other members respond to you? How did the group leader respond to you?

   c. Make up a list of specific problems that you might have that could interfere with your effectiveness in leading groups. For example, you may have an extreme need to be appreciated, which could determine your leadership style. You may have unresolved sexual conflicts, dependency needs, or exaggerated needs for power. Identify one area that you think you most need to explore as a potential barrier to effective leadership. Discuss this problem with your group. Although it may be unrealistic to expect a solution, you can talk about steps you could take to work on this problem.

8. Being a group member. What do you imagine that it would be like for you to be a member of an ongoing analytic group? What issues do you think you'd want to pursue in such a group? What kind of member do you think you'd be?

9. Role of group leader. Review the section in the textbook on the role of the analytic group leader. If you were to work within the framework of this model, what would this be like for you? Could you function within this model if it were your primary orientation? Why or why not?

10. Personal critique. Devote some time to a personal evaluation of the strengths and weaknesses of the analytic approach to group therapy. What specific techniques do you think are valuable? Why? What concepts could you draw on from this model in your work with groups, regardless of your orientation? What are the major contributions of the analytic model? What are the major limitations? With what kind of population do you think this model would be most appropriate? Least appropriate? Discuss

how the psychoanalytic theory forms the basis on which most of the other theories have developed—either as extensions of the model or as reactions against it.

<u>Reminder</u>: If you've not yet read the last two chapters in the textbook (Chapters 16 and 17), I suggest that you do so at this point. The case of a group in action and the comparison of theories will help you get an overall picture of how these theories are related. As you read and study the theory chapters, the last two chapters will give you an increased appreciation of how diverse theories can be applied to the different stages of a group's development.

7

ADLERIAN GROUP COUNSELING

PRECHAPTER PRIMER AND SELF-INVENTORY
FOR THE ADLERIAN APPROACH

Directions: Refer to page 58 for general directions. Indicate your position on each statement, using the following code:

5 = I strongly agree with this statement.

4 = I agree, in most respects, with this statement.

3 = I am undecided in my opinion about this statement.

2 = I disagree, in most respects, with this statement.

1 = I strongly disagree with this statement.

_____ 1. People are best understood by looking at their movement toward goals.

_____ 2. Group counseling is especially appropriate as an intervention because people are strongly motivated by social connectedness and because people cannot be fully understood apart from the social context.

_____ 3. Although people are influenced by their early childhood experiences, they are not passively shaped and determined by these experiences.

_____ 4. A useful focus in group counseling is on the interpersonal and social nature of a member's problems.

STAGES OF DEVELOPMENT OF THE ADLERIAN GROUP

Dimension	Initial Stage	Working Stage	Final Stage
Key developmental tasks and goals	Central developmental tasks are establishing empathy and creating acceptance, setting goals and making commitments, understanding one's current life-style, and exploring one's premises and assumptions. The psychological investigation that occurs in the group involves exploration of the family atmosphere and subjective interpretation of childhood events.	Members are helped to understand their beliefs, feelings, motives, and goals; they develop insight into their mistaken goals and self-defeating behaviors; they work through interpersonal conflicts; and they explore the beliefs behind their feelings. A goal is to create meaning and significance in life. Through group interaction, one's basic values and life-style become evident.	This is a time when members explore multiple alternatives to problems and make a commitment to change. They translate insights into action and make new decisions. A goal is to facilitate members' awareness of their mistaken notions through observation of fellow group members and reality testing.
Role of group leader and tasks	Main goal of the group leader is to establish a collaborative relationship and to decide with clients on the goals of the group. Leader's tasks include providing encouragement, offering support and tentative hypotheses of behavior, and helping members assess and clarify their problems. Role of leader is to observe social context of behavior in group and to model attentive listening, caring, sincerity, and confrontation. Leader helps members recognize and utilize their strengths.	Functions of leader at the working stage include interpreting early recollections and family patterns, helping members identify basic mistakes, helping members become aware of their own unique life-style, challenging members to deal with life tasks, and helping members summarize and integrate what they've learned so that they can make new plans. Leader assumes that members can best be understood by looking at their strivings and goals.	At the final stage the focus is on reeducation. Leader helps members challenge attitudes and encourages them to take risks and experiment with new behavior by translating their new ideas into actual behavior outside the group. Leader's tasks include helping members recognize their mistaken beliefs and become aware of their own self-defeating beliefs and behaviors.
Role of group members	Members state their goals and establish contracts. They are expected to be active in the group and begin to assume responsibility for the ways they want to change. Members begin to work on trust issues, which are important in the encouragement process and in developing good morale within the group.	Members become increasingly aware of their life-style. They analyze impact of family constellation; they also begin to recognize that they are responsible for their own behavior. Members provide support and challenge others so that they can explore their basic inferiority feelings. Participants learn to believe in themselves.	Members are expected to establish realistic goals. They see new options and more functional alternatives. They learn problem-solving and decision-making skills. This is a time of reorientation. Members encourage one another to redirect their goals along realistic lines.

Techniques	Basic listening skills are crucial at this time. Analysis and assessment of one's life-style and how it affects current functioning are conducted. Other techniques include questioning, reflection, and clarification.	Some of the techniques used at this stage are confrontation, interpretation, modeling, paraphrasing, encouragement, "catching oneself" in old patterns; acting "as if," and teaching.	Basic procedures at the final stage consist of encouraging members to act and to change. Contracts are reestablished, and role-playing techniques are used to help members reorient their goals. There is a continuation of the encouragement process.
Questions to consider	How can you, as a leader, establish a collaborative relationship with the members? Since Adlerians are concerned with the ways that people strive for significance, how can the group itself be used to help members understand the ways they find meaning and the ways they meet the challenge of life? How well are the members dealing with current life tasks? Why are the members seeking this group now? What are some themes to look for in obtaining the life-style assessment of members? • parental influences • family information • memories of each sibling • role in the family • earliest recollections • critical turning points in life	What are the values of focusing on clients' beliefs and motives with the intention of helping them develop insight into their mistaken goals? How can early recollections and family patterns be interpreted in light of the members' current behavior in the group situation? Leaders might think of this question in helping members become aware of their life-style: under what circumstances does the person acquire a particular life-style, and how is this being maintained currently? What are some techniques of helping members catch themselves in old patterns and begin to behave in new and more effective ways?	How can members be challenged to make a commitment to change? How can insights be translated into action? What are some ways that members can apply problem-solving and decision-making skills acquired in the group to actual behavior outside of the group? To what degree are the members behaving as active and autonomous beings as opposed to acting as victims of fate? To what extent have the members become actively involved with other people and developed a new life-style through relationships? Can members summarize changes in attitudes, beliefs, goals, and behaviors? Are they feeling encouraged to take risks by acting on these changes?

Reactions: Summarize your reactions to the Adlerian perspective on group developmental stages. What do you like most? least? What aspects of this approach would you incorporate in your style of group leadership?

_____ 5. In family therapy a useful approach is teaching family members how to recognize issues that are dividing them, how to compromise, and how to make responsible decisions.

_____ 6. Recalling one's earliest memories is an extremely important group-work technique.

_____ 7. People have a basic need to be superior—that is, to overcome feelings of inferiority.

_____ 8. Each person develops a unique life-style, which should be examined in group sessions.

_____ 9. The group counselor's and the group member's goals must concur.

_____ 10. An analysis of each member's family constellation is essential to successful group work.

SUMMARY OF BASIC ASSUMPTIONS AND KEY CONCEPTS OF THE ADLERIAN APPROACH

1. The underlying assumptions of the Adlerian approach are as follows: humans are primarily social beings, motivated by social forces; they are shaped largely by social interactions; conscious, not unconscious, processes determine personality and behavior; people are creative, active, and autonomous beings, not the victims of fate.

2. All people have basic feelings of inferiority that motivate them to strive for superiority, mastery, power, and perfection.

3. People seek to overcome helplessness through compensation. People's life-style comprises unique behaviors and habits they develop in striving for power, meaning, and personal goals; their life-style, which is formed early in life as compensation for specific feelings of inferiority, also shapes their views of the world and of themselves.

4. Therapists should encourage group members to become actively involved with other people and develop a new life-style through relationships.

5. Therapists should challenge clients to have faith and hope and develop the courage to face life actively and choose the kind of life they want. This is done largely by living <u>as if</u> we were the way we want to be.

EXERCISES AND ACTIVITIES FOR THE ADLERIAN APPROACH

1. Adlerians use a technique known as "the question." This consists of asking a client "How would you be different if _____?" The end of the sentence refers to being free of a problem or a symptom. For example, if you were troubled with migraine headaches, you would be asked how you'd

be different if you no longer had these headaches. Apply this question to a specific problem you have. Explore how your life might be different without this problem. How do you think your problem may be useful to you? Are you "rewarded" for some of your symptoms?

2. What are some of your earliest memories? Describe them in your group. Are they mainly joyful or painful memories? What value do you see in the Adlerian technique of having clients recall their earliest memories? Can you think of ways to use this technique in groups you may lead?

3. Adlerians place emphasis on birth order and family constellation. Share with your group members what it was like to be the first-born child, or the last-born, or the middle child, or the only child. What does your group think are the advantages and disadvantages of each of these positions? Discussing these topics can help group members get acquainted with one another, as well as stir up old memories.

4. According to Adler, we all strive for superiority to compensate for inferiority. How does this apply to you? In what ways do you feel inferior? Do you see yourself as having developed certain strengths that characterize the way you present yourself to others? In describing your life-style consider such questions as What makes you unique? How do you strive for power? When do you feel the most powerful? What are the goals that you most strive for? What do you most often tell others about yourself on a first meeting? How do you typically present yourself?

5. Adlerian therapists often ask group members to live "as if" they were the person they wanted to be. For example, you may want to be far more creative than you are now. Assume that you are more creative, and then describe yourself to your group. What are some ways that you can think of to use this "as if" technique in a group? What value do you see in it?

6. Adlerians center on "basic mistakes," or faulty assumptions, that people make about themselves. These mistaken ideas lead to self-defeating behavior. For example, you may believe that to feel successful you must be perfect. Since you'll never feel perfect, you will constantly put yourself under needless stress and experience little joy over any accomplishments. Select what you consider to be one faulty assumption that you have made about yourself or the world. Discuss in your group how this affects you. If you were to change this assumption, how might your life be different?

7. What is your personal evaluation of the Adlerian approach to group therapy? What do you see as the major strengths and limitations of the model? What concepts do you like most? Like least? Which Adlerian group-therapy methods would you use?

8. What are the cross-cultural implications of using Adlerian concepts and techniques in group work? Are there any ethnic or cultural groups that you think Adlerian groups would not be suited for? For what types of population do you think Adlerian group approaches have the most relevance?

71

LIFE-STYLE ASSESSMENT

   As mentioned in the textbook, Adlerians often begin a group with a
structured interview to obtain information about the family constellation,
early recollections, life goals, and childhood experiences of the members.
If you have a basic grasp of the concepts of Adlerian psychology, you can
develop your own inventory for getting some of this information. Although
there are formal formats for the life-style questionnaire, the purpose of
this exercise is to provide you with the experience of gathering data about
yourself that you could use if you were a member of a group. It is hoped
that by practicing on yourself you will gain some ideas for what you might
want to look for in interviews with the members of the groups you will lead.
Answer the following questions as directly, simply, and honestly as you can
under the assumption that you would be interested in joining an Adlerian
group as a member.

1. What is your main reason for seeking a group?

2. How well are you dealing with current life tasks? In addressing this
    question, think of the following areas: leisure, friendship, being a
    part of a family, relationships with the opposite sex, meaning in life,
    being a parent, adjustment to work, finding hobbies, your feelings about
    self, and any other areas you think of.

3. How have your parents influenced your life? Take each parent and answer
    questions such as the following:

    • Describe the parent. What kind of person was he or she?

    • What ambitions did the parent have for you?

    • What relationship did this parent have to each child in the family?

    • What were your main feelings toward the parent when you were growing
      up in your family? What are your feelings toward him or her now?

    • In what ways are you similar/different from the parent?

    • How would you describe the relationship your parents had with each
      other?

4. What other family information do you recall? What about your family do
    you think is relevant to the person who you are now?

5. Describe your brothers and sisters (from the oldest to the youngest).
    What do you remember about each sibling? How would you compare your-
    self with each sibling? Which sibling is most like you, and in which
    respect? Which is most different from you, and in which way? How would
    you describe your position in the family? What expectations did you
    have for each sibling? What were their expectations for you?

6. What are your earliest recollections? What specific incidents stand
    out for you? Do you recall how you felt in selected situations? Can you
    recall any reactions that you had in these situations?

7. What do you recall about your growth and development? In addressing this
    question, think about specific areas such as physical development, major

changes in childhood and adolescence, social development, sexual development, childhood fears, ambitions and goals, special talents, assets, liabilities, school experiences, and work experiences.

8. Can you identify any basic mistakes (mistaken self-defeating perceptions) that you acquired in childhood or adolescence? Examples: Any faulty generalizations, such as "Nobody really cares about me." "I am always singled out as the one nobody likes." Any denial of your value as a person, such as "I am basically unlovable." "I will never accomplish what I want to in life." Any misperceptions of reality: "Since people expect so much of me, I'll never measure up, and I'll always be frustrated."

9. Attempt to write a brief summary of key characteristics of your family constellation and your early recollections. From what you know of yourself, what might you select to explore in a group?

10. What do you see as your major assets? What about your liabilities? What would you most want to change in your past if you could relive your childhood?

8

PSYCHODRAMA

PRECHAPTER PRIMER AND SELF-INVENTORY
FOR PSYCHODRAMA

Directions: Refer to page 58 for general directions. Indicate your position on each statement, using the following code:

5 = I strongly agree with this statement.

4 = I agree, in most respects, with this statement.

3 = I am undecided in my opinion about this statement.

2 = I disagree, in most respects, with this statement.

1 = I strongly disagree with this statement.

_____ 1. There is therapeutic value in releasing pent-up feelings, even if this process does not lead to changing external situations.

_____ 2. Much can be learned from acting out one's conflicts, rather than merely talking about them.

_____ 3. The use of fantasy techniques in a group can increase members' awareness of themselves.

_____ 4. Group members can learn a great deal about themselves by observing and experiencing the psychodramas of other members.

_____ 5. It is important to "warm up" a group before moving into action.

_____ 6. Role playing one's own role <u>and</u> the role of a significant other person can increase one's awareness of oneself.

_____ 7. After intensive group work, members should share their feelings and discuss how they perceive the work.

_____ 8. A group leader should both encourage catharsis and help members understand emotional experiences.

_____ 9. Group members (protagonists) should always have the right to choose what conflict they will portray, and they should have the right to say that they do not want to move in a given direction.

_____ 10. Unless a group is cohesive, it is unlikely that members will risk role-playing important problems.

SUMMARY OF BASIC ASSUMPTIONS AND KEY CONCEPTS OF PSYCHODRAMA

1. Psychodrama frees people from old feelings so that they are able to develop new ways of responding to problems. Spontaneity, creativity, fantasy, and role playing are essential elements of psychodrama.

2. Psychodrama emphasizes enacting or reenacting events (anticipated or past) as though they were occurring in the present.

3. Feelings are released; participants gain insight and are provided with the opportunity to test reality. Group members suggest alternatives for action.

4. The psychodrama director's tasks include being a producer, catalyst/facilitator, and observer/analyzer.

5. A basic assumption underlying psychodrama is that members of the group can benefit therapeutically in vicarious ways by identifying with a protagonist in a psychodrama.

6. Psychodrama has three phases: the warm-up process, the action phase, and the discussion phase.

7. Psychodrama has many uses in working with a family as a group. Members can step into the shoes of other family members, and through role-reversal techniques can develop empathy as well as new ways of responding.

8. Psychodrama places importance on the past, present, <u>and</u> future; the past can come to life when it is brought into the here and now, as can the future.

STAGES OF DEVELOPMENT OF THE PSYCHODRAMA GROUP

Dimension	Initial Stage	Working Stage	Final Stage
Key developmental tasks and goals	The key task of the initial stage is the warm-up, which fosters spontaneity. This warm-up period develops a readiness to participate in the experience. Emphasis is on forming common bonds by identifying common experiences.	A major task of psychodrama is to facilitate expression of feelings in a spontaneous and dramatic way through role playing. Full expression of conflicts leads to new awareness of problems. During this phase a corrective emotional experience occurs through enactment and catharsis, leading to insight. Reality testing can follow, using a variety of techniques.	Major tasks of this phase are working through conflict situations by behavioral practice and by getting feedback, developing a sense of mastery over certain problems, receiving support from the group, and integrating what is learned into life outside the group.
Role of group leader and tasks	Director introduces the nature and purpose of psychodrama and warms up the audience (group) using techniques. Members are briefly interviewed and asked what kind of situation they would be willing to work on. A protagonist is selected. Director's main task is to create a climate of support and prepare the group drama. Director may select a theme (such as loneliness, dealing with intimacy, and so on) that the group can focus on.	During this phase the director's task is to encourage members to enact scenes involving conflicts. Emphasis is on action, keeping the members focused on the present, and helping them to fully express feelings. Director facilitates and interprets the action and encourages spontaneity and expression. Director brings other members forward to take the parts of other significant figures in the protagonist's drama. Director helps these auxiliary egos learn their roles.	After the main action, director helps protagonist integrate what has occurred. Director asks for feedback and support from other members; in this way, all members get involved in the psychodrama. Care is taken so that those who participated in the psychodrama are not left hanging. Director may summarize the session and help everyone to integrate the psychodramatic occurrences.
Role of group members	Members discuss goals, get acquainted with one another, and participate in exercises to get them focused. Members may decide on a theme of common interest, which in turn leads to the selection of a protagonist. Members decide what personal issues they will explore.	Members define in concrete terms a situation to be enacted; they reconstruct an anxiety-causing event from the past or one anticipated in the future. The members fantasize and express themselves as fully as possible, both verbally and nonverbally. Members serve as auxiliary egos for the protagonist.	Members share with the protagonist feelings they had as the enactment took place. The sharing is done in a personal way, not an analytical way. Members give feedback to the protagonist, and they offer support. Members share the personal experiences that the psychodrama reminded them of.

	Techniques
Techniques	The warm-up period may be directed or undirected. Warm-up techniques include the use of guided fantasy, dance, and music; the use of artistic materials; the sharing of drawings; and brief interviews of each member. A wide range of action-oriented techniques are used. These include self-presentation, presentation of the other, role reversal, soliloquy, doubling, the mirror technique, dream work, and future projection. After the action phase of a psychodrama, certain closure techniques may be used, such as sharing techniques, the magic shop, feedback, repeating the drama with new approaches, and discussing alternative behaviors and possible solutions to problems.

Techniques

The warm-up period may be directed or undirected. Warm-up techniques include the use of guided fantasy, dance, and music; the use of artistic materials; the sharing of drawings; and brief interviews of each member.

A wide range of action-oriented techniques are used. These include self-presentation, presentation of the other, role reversal, soliloquy, doubling, the mirror technique, dream work, and future projection.

After the action phase of a psychodrama, certain closure techniques may be used, such as sharing techniques, the magic shop, feedback, repeating the drama with new approaches, and discussing alternative behaviors and possible solutions to problems.

Questions to consider

As a leader of a psychodrama, how can you tap into the creativity that exists within the group? Are you alert to connecting up one person's work with others in the group as a way of promoting group cohesion?

What are some ways that trust can be established, and how can members be encouraged to participate in role-playing?

How can the members best be prepared for taking an active part in the group? How can you help them to overcome their resistance to role-playing?

What are some ways of finding themes and concerns that most members share? Once these common problems are identified, how can you facilitate the group so that members can work these issues together?

As the group progresses, you might ask yourself such questions as:

• Do I have the courage to experiment with methods even though I do not know the possible outcome?

• Do I trust my clinical hunches to try out a technique and to flow with what the member produces?

• Do I have control of the group without dominating it? Are the members able to express their spontaneity and get involved?

• Am I able to orchestrate all the members so that everyone plays a vital part in the group process?

• Is everyone in the group involved in the process? Are some members working silently, but not expressing verbally their thoughts and feelings? How can they be encouraged to bring out their reactions?

After a psychodrama, does the member have an opportunity to put into words what he or she has experienced and learned? Is care taken so that the person is not left feeling unfinished? Are some steps taken to help the member translate what was learned in the group into situations in his or her everyday life?

After catharsis, how can the members be helped to give words to their emotional experience? How can a cognitive component be integrated with emotional work? How can member see a link between past emotional issues and options for change of current behavior?

As a leader, are you alert to ways that others in the group might have been affected by a person's work?

How can you help members attain a vision of changes desired in the future? And how can this be practiced?

Reactions: Summarize your reactions to the psychodramatic perspective on group developmental stages. What do you like most? least? What aspects of this approach would you incorporate in your style of leadership?

EXERCISES AND ACTIVITIES FOR PSYCHODRAMA

Rationale

Psychodrama is based on the rationale that therapeutic work is enhanced by dealing with problems as though they are occurring in the present. The following exercises, activities, and problems are designed to give you some experience with psychodrama; experiment with them as much as possible in your group. These exercises will help you directly experience your concerns, release feelings, and gain insight. They will also help you increase your awareness of others' experiences and thus help you to develop more sensitivity to others.
As you work through these activities in small groups, think of imaginative ways to modify them.

Exercises

1. You are setting up a psychodrama for your group. What warm-up techniques will you use? Practice these techniques in your group, and get feedback on your effectiveness from fellow group members.

2. You encourage a member of the group you are leading to role-play a situation involving a conflict with her father. She says: "I won't role-play, because that seems phony. Role playing always makes me self-conscious. Is it OK if I just talk about my problem with my father instead?" How would you respond? (You might act this out in your own class group; have one person role-play the reluctant member, and another person the leader. Group members should take turns playing the roles, so that several ways of working with reluctance can be demonstrated.)

3. As a group leader, how would you encourage members to select significant personal issues to explore in a psychodrama without coercing them to participate?

4. Assume that a member tells you that he'd like to get involved in a particular psychodrama because he has a lot of anger stored up against women. He tells you, however, that he is afraid that, if he does get involved, he will lose control and perhaps even make the women in the group the target of his rage. He is afraid he might "go crazy" if he takes the lid off his feelings. How would you respond?

5. A man in your group wants to explore his relationship with his daughter, which he describes as being strained. How would you proceed with him? What specific techniques might you suggest? What would you expect to accomplish with these procedures?

6. One of the women in the group describes her conflicts with her daughter as follows: "My daughter tells me that I simply don't understand what it's like to be 16. We fight continually, and the more I try to get her to do what I think is right, the more defiant she becomes. I simply don't know where to begin. How can I reach her?" Act out the above situation in your class or small group. Assume you are the leader, and get another person in class to role-play the mother. Consider trying these techniques:

- role reversal (mother becomes the daughter)

- self-presentation (mother presents her side of this conflict)

- presentation of the other (mother presents the daughter's side)

- soliloquy (mother verbalizes uncensored feelings/thoughts)

What other techniques can you think of to practice in this situation?

7. Assume that the woman in the above case is role-playing with another member, who is playing the daughter. All of a sudden the mother stops and says: "I'm stuck; I just don't know what to say now. Whenever she gets that hurt look in her eyes and begins to cry, I feel rotten, guilty, and I freeze up. What can I do now?" In this instance, try the double technique (another member becomes an auxiliary ego and stands behind the mother and speaks for her). You could also use the multiple double technique (where two or more people represent different facets of the mother). One double might represent the guilty mother who attempts to placate her daughter, and the other double could be the firm mother who deals directly with the daughter's manipulation.

8. One of the women in your group seems aloof and judgmental. Members in the group pick up nonverbal cues such as frowning, glances and positioning of her head, and other indications of superiority. She says that people outside of the group have the same impression of her, yet she does not feel judgmental, nor does she perceive herself as others do. Assume that this woman wants to explore this issue and use the mirror technique. Someone in your class group can play the role of the woman who is perceived as aloof and judgmental, and you or another member can imitate her posture, gestures, and speech. Can you think of other techniques to help this woman explore the discrepancy between her self-image and the view others have of her?

9. Think of a situation in which the use of the magic shop technique would be appropriate. Think of another case in which you'd be likely to employ the future projection technique. If possible, set up these situations in your class/group, and get practice using these techniques.

10. Select a personal problem that you are concerned about or a relationship that you'd like to understand better. (You must be willing to share this problem in your class/group. If dealing with a current problem seems too threatening, consider working on a past problem that you have resolved.) Then set up a psychodrama in your group in which you are the protagonist. This exercise, if done properly, will give you a sense of what it's like to be a member of a psychodrama group.

QUESTIONS FOR DISCUSSION AND EVALUATION

1. What problems, if any, would you predict for yourself as a participant in a psychodrama? What about being a leader/director of one?

2. What are the advantages of psychodrama's action-oriented methods, in which members actually act out and experience their conflicts as opposed

to merely talking about them? What limitations or disadvantages do you see in this approach?

3. Psychodrama consists of verbally and nonverbally releasing pent-up feelings such as anger, hatred, despair, and so on. Do you feel able to deal with the release of your intense feelings? Have you already experienced a similar type of catharsis? Do you think that you have the knowledge and the skills to effectively deal with people who express such intense emotions? Could you deal with the emotional effects catharsis may trigger in other group members?

4. How can cognitive work be incorporated in the emotional aspects of psychodrama? In your view, if a leader discontinues the helping process after people have expressed pent-up emotions, is this enough to lead to insight and behavioral change? How might you help people progress by thinking about what they've experienced and putting it into a cognitive framework so that meaning can be added to experience?

5. Do you see any limitations to using psychodrama as an exclusive method in a group, without combining it with the concepts and techniques of other approaches?

6. Do you think that psychodrama has equal therapeutic value for people from all cultures? If not, for what ethnic and cultural groups do you think psychodrama is best suited? least suited?

7. What are some possible psychological risks associated with psychodrama? How would you caution group members before they participated in a psychodrama? How do you think the potential dangers can be reduced?

8. If you were using psychodrama, what steps would you take to see that members were not left hanging with unfinished business? What would you do if a group member were left very open to intense emotions at the end of a group meeting?

9

THE EXISTENTIAL APPROACH

PRECHAPTER PRIMER AND SELF-INVENTORY FOR
THE EXISTENTIAL APPROACH

Directions: Refer to page 58 for general directions. Indicate your position on each statement, using the following code:

5 = I strongly agree with this statement.

4 = I agree, in most repects, with this statement.

3 = I am undecided in my opinion about this statement.

2 = I disagree, in most respects, with this statement.

1 = I strongly disagree with this statement.

_____ 1. Group work should focus on the subjective aspects of a member's
experience.

_____ 2. The central issues in counseling and therapy are freedom, responsibility, and the anxiety that accompanies being both free and responsible.

_____ 3. Anxiety and guilt are not necessarily disorders to be cured, for
these are a part of the human condition.

_____ 4. Being aware of death gives meaning to life and makes each person
realize that he or she is ultimately alone.

_____ 5. Group therapy's basic task is to expand consciousness and thus extend freedom.

STAGES OF DEVELOPMENT OF THE EXISTENTIAL GROUP

Dimension	Initial Stage	Working Stage	Final Stage
Key developmental tasks and goals	Focus is on how members perceive and experience their world; thus, approach is experiential and subjective. Main goal is to increase awareness of options in order to widen everyone's freedom. Initial task of a group is making a commitment to explore personally meaningful and significant issues concerning human struggles.	Members explore a wide range of universal human concerns such as loneliness, the anxiety of recognizing that one is free to make choices and that freedom is always accompanied by responsibility, the meaning of life and death, and so on. Participants consider alternative ways of dealing with issues they are facing. Emphasis is on taking responsibility now for the way one chooses to be. Focus is on self-discovery, which often leads to giving up defenses and living authentically.	Group counseling or therapy is seen as an "invitation to change." Members are challenged to re-create themselves. In the group, they have opportunities to evaluate their life and to choose how they will change. Toward the end of a group, termination is another issue to face, for the ending of a group brings on anxiety. "Death" of a group must be dealt with fully.
Role of group leader and tasks	Leader's tasks are to confront members with the issue of dealing with freedom and responsibility and to challenge them to recognize that, regardless of the limits of choosing, there is always some element of choice in life.	Emphasis is on creating an "I/Thou" relationship, which entails the leader's full presence. Leader's task is to be there as a person for the members; he or she embarks on an unknown journey with the members and is open to where they will go together. Leaders must understand and adopt the members' subjective world. Leaders also engage in self-disclosure and model authentic behavior.	At the final stage of a group, leader challenges members to go into the world and be active. Leader helps members integrate and consolidate what they've learned in the group, so that the maximum transfer can occur. Rather than "doing therapy," leader lives it through the openness of ongoing existential encounters with the members.
Role of group members	Members always have a part in the group process. They look at who and what they are; they clarify their identity and make decisions concerning how they can achieve authenticity. Members decide what they will explore in the group.	Members decide what struggles or existential concerns they will share. Typical concerns include changing roles, creating new identities when old identities are no longer meaningful, value conflicts, emptiness, dealing with loneliness, and working on the fear of freedom and responsibility.	In order to change, members must go out into the world and act. Since they are responsible for their own life, they decide if and how they want to live differently. If a group is successful, members achieve an authentic identity and become aware of choices that can lead to action.

Technique	There are no prescribed techniques, and therapeutic procedures can be borrowed from many approaches. More than a group leader's technique or skill, the leader's attitude and behavior are crucial for the group's results. Group leaders are not viewed as technical experts who apply therapeutic treatment plans. There is no assessment, nor is there a predetermined treatment plan for the group to follow.	Emphasis is not so much on doing therapy by using techniques; rather, it is on creating an "I/Thou" relationship and being fully present. Thus, leaders may work with dreams, they may work with the current interaction in the group, they may explore the past with members, and they may be both supportive and challenging. Emphasis is on constructive confrontation, so that members can learn how to confront themselves.	Since group counseling or therapy is seen as a spontaneous encounter between members (and between members and the leader), the leader is free to draw on a diverse range of techniques from many other therapies. Although the focus is on the encounter that occurs in the group, specific techniques can be developed to challenge the members to recognize the choices they have and the decisions to make a new life.
Questions to consider	An existential group can be described as people making a commitment to begin and to continue a lifelong journey of self-exploration. Ask yourself the degree to which you are willing to embark on this journey for self-awareness. Are you willing to do in your own life what you ask your members to do? Are you able to experience the suffering and despair that is sometimes necessary? How do you deal with anxiety in your own life? Do you face it, or do you try to avoid it? How might this affect the way you lead a group?	To what degree are you able to be present for those in your group? Are you willing to travel down whatever paths a member might lead you? Can you adopt the members' subjective view of the world? Do you model in the group those attitudes and behaviors you hope the members will develop? What do you model? Are you able to borrow techniques from other approaches and apply them to the struggles of members? In using techniques, is it done within the context of the relationship that you have established with members and in the climate of trust?	Are the members willing to take action? Are they able to act on what they have learned? Are they committed to making changes in their life? How will they make certain changes? Are the members able to see that they do have choices? that there is a price to pay for acting on their choices? that they must choose for themselves in the face of uncertainty? Are they moving in the direction of trusting their decisions and relying less upon others to decide for them? Are members more aware of the options for action available to them? Are they now better able to cope with the anxiety that comes with freedom than when they entered the group?

Reactions: Summarize your reactions to the existential perspective on group developmental stages. What do you like most? least? What aspects of this approach would you incorporate in your style of leadership?

_____ 6. The meaning of death should be examined in group-therapy sessions.

_____ 7. The group leader's function is not to tell members what life should mean to them but to encourage them to discover this meaning for themselves.

_____ 8. An inauthentic existence consists of living a life as outlined and determined by others, rather than a life based on one's own inner experience.

_____ 9. The effective counselor is less concerned with "doing therapy" than with living therapy by being with another.

_____ 10. Therapists' major tasks are fostering self-disclosure, creating "I/Thou" relationships, and providing a model for clients.

SUMMARY OF BASIC ASSUMPTIONS AND KEY CONCEPTS OF THE EXISTENTIAL APPROACH

1. The therapist focuses on independent choice and freedom, the potential within humans to find their own way, and the search for identity and self-actualization.

2. People become what they choose to become, and, although there are factors that restrict choices, self-determination is ultimately the basis of their uniqueness as individuals.

3. Group-therapy work should emphasize such themes as meaning in life, guilt, anxiety, responsibility, death, and one's ultimate aloneness.

4. The therapist's ultimate goal is enabling clients to be free and responsible for the direction of their own life. Therefore, the clients are largely responsible for what occurs in therapy.

5. The therapist's major tasks are to grasp the subjective world of their clients and to establish authentic relationships in which clients can work on understanding themselves and their choices more fully.

6. Group leaders do not behave in rigid or prescribed ways, for they can't predict the exact direction or content of any group. Leaders are not technical experts who carry out treatment plans with specialized techniques; rather, they establish real relationships with the members of the group.

7. The presence of the leader, or the leader's willingness to be there for others and confront them when appropriate, is a major characteristic of the effective group. Group leaders must be willing to take responsibility for their own thinking, feeling, and judging. They are present as persons with the members, for they become active agents in the group.

8. Existential theory does not aim at "curing sick people," because it holds that it isn't possible to "cure" or to "remove" certain basic

human conditions. Existential crises are seen as a part of living and not something to be remedied. These crises frequently concern the meaning of life, anxiety and guilt, and the fear of choosing and accepting responsibility for one's choices. Because these "crises" aren't necessarily pathological, they can't be externally alleviated; they should be lived through and understood in the context of a group.

EXERCISES AND ACTIVITIES FOR THE EXISTENTIAL APPROACH

Rationale

The existential approach does not provide a ready-made set of techniques for group practitioners. It is more an orientation to group counseling than a system of therapeutic procedures. Practitioners can adhere to the existential perspective and at the same time use many of the other therapeutic techniques.

What follows are examples of activities that are in some way related to existential themes. Use these exercises both on your own and in your group/ class, and then you'll have a better idea how to integrate existential concepts into your leadership style. Think about what you can learn about both yourself and group processes through these exercises.

Exercises

1. Self-awareness. Group members often say that they are afraid of learning too much about themselves. They may accept the notion that "ignorance is bliss" or "what you don't know won't hurt you." What is your position on this? Are you clearly open to learning all that you can about yourself? Or do you have reservations about expanding your self-awareness? What concerns might you have about opening doors to your life that are now closed? Discuss these questions in your class/group.

2. Freedom and responsibility. Freedom of choice entails accepting the responsibility for influencing the direction of your life. Being free means that, as long as you are alive, you are making choices about who it is you are becoming. Do you believe that you are what you are now largely as a result of your choices, or do you feel that you are the product of circumstances? What are some major choices that you've made that have been crucial to your present development? Discuss some of these crucial decisions in your group. How do you imagine your life would be different now if you had decided differently?

3. Anxiety. Anxiety is not only an impetus to change but also a result of recognizing that you are responsible for your choices. What kind of anxiety have you experienced in terms of making key life decisions? How do you tend to manage your anxiety: by directly facing the consequences of your choices? by attempting to make others responsible for you? by avoiding making choices? by attempting to deny reality? Do you agree with the existential notion that anxiety produces growth? How well do you manage anxiety in your own life? In what situations do you experience the most anxiety?

4. Death. How well are you able to accept the fact of your own death? Do you see any relationship between how you view death and the degree to which you are living fully now? In order to clarify your thoughts and feelings about death and to examine how death affects the way you live, try some of the following exercises in your class or group.

    a. What do you think the significant people in your life would write on your tombstone? What would you like them to say?

    b. Write the eulogy you'd like delivered at your funeral. Bring it to the group and share it with other members.

    c. Assume that you knew you were going to die within 24 hours. What would you most like to do during these final hours? What does this say about your values?

    d. Tell others in your group what you'd most like to accomplish before you die.

    e. If you have experienced the loss of someone close to you, consider sharing what this has been like for you. What did you learn about yourself through this experience?

5. Meaning in life. Confronting our mortality makes us think about how meaningful our life is. In your group, let yourself imagine a typical day in your life five years ago. What was it like, and what were you like then? Are there any major differences between your life then and now? Share some of the most significant changes you've made over the past five years with others in your group. Then, project yourself five years into the future. What do you hope you'll be like then? What do you fear you might be like then? Explore in your group what you are experiencing in your life that contributes to or detracts from a meaningful existence.

6. Authenticity. The existential perspective stresses that affirming ourselves is an ongoing process. We are authentic if we face the anxiety of choosing for ourselves and accept the consequences of our choices. Inauthentic people allow others to determine who and what they are. Discuss some crucial incidents in your own personal struggles to define yourself. Consider some of these questions as you construct your personal-identity road map:

    • Who am I? What has contributed to the way I am?

    • What roles have I typically played? How have I seen myself?

    • What choices did I make? What choices did others make for me?

    • Have I lost contact with myself by looking to others for answers and direction? Do I trust others more than myself?

    • How has my life been shaped by past actions, people, influences, and so on?

    • What more do I want from my life? What kind of identity am I searching for?

- If some of the elements that I depend on for a sense of my
  identity were taken away, what would I be like?

7. Loneliness. Share in your group some ways that each member has experienced loneliness. Can you recall the time in your life when you felt most alone? What was this like for you? Select a poem, a picture, or an excerpt from a book that captures the loneliness you have felt at some time in your life. Bring this to the group and share it.

8. Creative solitude. Existentialists believe that, unless we can enjoy solitude creatively, we cannot develop genuine intimacy with others. Do you make time for yourself to be alone? When you are alone, what is this generally like for you? Do you welcome it or flee from it? Select a song, poem, poster, or picture that represents peaceful solitude to you. In what ways might you want to learn how to enjoy time alone?

9. Role and functions of the group leader. The existential approach emphasizes the role of the leader not so much as a doer of therapy but as a person to be fully present with the group members. Discuss in your group the degree to which you feel personally equipped to challenge others to look at the important issues in life. For instance, do you feel ready to challenge others to look at the choices they've made as well as the ones now open to them? Have you done this in your own life? Could you be psychologically with another person who was exploring a life/death issue? Have you been willing to face such issues in your life?

10. Personal evaluation and critique. In your group or class, explore the concepts of the existential approach you find most valuable. What would you borrow from this approach? What are the limitations of the approach? What disadvantages do you see in limiting yourself strictly to an existential orientation? Do you think this perspective has something to offer every client? For what kinds of person do you think it is the most appropriate? How are you able to relate in a personal way to the existential approach? What are the therapeutic techniques from other models that you'd use to apply existential concepts in the groups you lead or will lead?

10

THE PERSON-CENTERED APPROACH

PRECHAPTER PRIMER AND SELF-INVENTORY FOR THE
PERSON-CENTERED APPROACH

Directions: Refer to page 58 for general directions. Indicate your position on each statement, using the following code:

5 = I strongly agree with this statement.

4 = I agree, in most respects, with this statement.

3 = I am undecided in my opinion about this statement.

2 = I disagree, in most respects, with this statement.

1 = I strongly disagree with this statement.

_____ 1. The group members, not the leader, have the primary responsibility for the direction the group takes.

_____ 2. The attitudes of acceptance, empathy, warmth, respect, genuineness, and positive regard are both necessary and sufficient for
therapeutic change to occur.

_____ 3. A leader's direction is not necessary for a group to move in a constructive direction.

_____ 4. A major function of the group leader is to establish a climate of
trust in the group.

_____ 5. A group leader can be effective without attending to transference.

_____ 6. Self-disclosure on the leader's part tends to increase trust and self-disclosure on the part of the members.

_____ 7. Group members should be involved in choosing the techniques or structured exercises used in the group.

_____ 8. The group leader is more a facilitator than a director.

_____ 9. Directive intervention by the leader can interfere with the group process.

_____ 10. Group leaders should avoid giving advice.

SUMMARY OF BASIC ASSUMPTIONS AND KEY CONCEPTS OF THE PERSON-CENTERED APPROACH

1. Clients are basically trustworthy and have the potential for self-direction. The group can become aware of problems and the means to resolve them if the group facilitator encourages them to explore present feelings and thoughts.

2. Because the group has the potential for self-direction, there is a minimum of direction on the leader's part, for this tends to undermine respect for the group members.

3. External measures such as diagnosis, testing, interpretation, advice giving, and probing for information are not used. Instead, therapy comprises active listening, reflection and clarification, and understanding the inner world of the clients.

4. The therapeutic relationship between group leader and members helps the members grow and change. The therapist must reflect warmth, acceptance, respect, caring, and empathy and must not be judgmental.

QUESTIONS FOR DISCUSSION AND EVALUATION

1. Group goals. Do you agree with Rogers' contention that the group has the capacity to move in constructive directions without structure, direction, and active intervention on the leader's part? Why or why not? What are the implications for practice if you accept this assumption? Do you agree that group members are the ones to formulate specific goals?

2. Attending and listening. How well do you listen and attend? What gets in your way of fully attending to others? How can you improve your attending skills?

3. Empathy. What is your understanding of empathy? How can you become empathic? What are the barriers to this? Do you expect to have the problem of overidentification—losing your own identity by immersing yourself in another's world? What part does leader self-disclosure play in advanced levels of empathy? How can you improve your ability to develop appropri-

STAGES OF DEVELOPMENT OF THE PERSON-CENTERED GROUP

Dimension	Initial Stage	Working Stage	Final Stage
Key developmental tasks and goals	Early stages of group are characterized by some floundering and a search for direction. Typically, members present a socially acceptable facade or reveal the "safer" sides of themselves; they describe themselves in a "there-and-then" manner. There is a milling around and a sense of confusion concerning the purpose and the function of the group. A key task is to build trust.	Negative feelings often surface over the lack of leadership. Then, a more accepting and trusting climate may prevail. Members show more of themselves, cohesion develops, and members find support in the group. Some confrontation occurs, especially when members sense that others are not being genuine. False fronts give way to a real expression of self.	The group develops a healing capacity, and members are able to move forward based on the support offered. Members develop self-acceptance; they offer feedback to one another in a climate of honesty, and a sense of community develops. Behavior changes are noticed in the group. Members show increased ease in expressing their feelings, and they gain insight into how they relate to others.
Role of group leader and tasks	Facilitator's main role is to grant freedom to members to develop a structure of their own. Leader places responsibility on members for the direction they will take. Group leaders have the job of being sensitive to whatever direction is taken by the group and following that lead. Leader is concerned with creating a climate that is psychologically safe for the members. Leader's role is to be without a role. Central function is to help members interact honestly.	A central task of the leader is to adopt an empathic viewpoint; it is important that members feel deeply understood and cared for. Leader needs to accept negative as well as positive feelings. Leader needs to share own ongoing feelings and reactions with the group. Leader listens actively, reflects, clarifies, summarizes, links members' statements, demonstrates respect, and also shows acceptance and caring for members.	Central role of leader is to help members express how they have experienced this group and to encourage honest feedback. Leader should help members apply what they have learned in the group to life outside of it.
Role of group members	Members are expected to develop their own goals and decide for themselves how they will spend their time together. At first members are rather confused and search for a structure. They are resistant to sharing personally significant material.	Members decide what they will reveal about themselves; they express feelings to others in the group. They offer both support and challenge to others; they give and receive feedback. Members at this stage are usually willing to express immediate interpersonal feelings of both a positive and a negative nature. Self-exploration occurs on a deeper level.	Members move from playing roles to being real, from being relatively closed to being open and able to tolerate some ambiguity, from being out of contact with internal and subjective experience to being aware of the ongoing subjective process, from looking for external answers to looking inward for direction.

Techniques	Person-centered leaders tend to avoid using planned exercises and techniques to "get a group moving." They rely on the capacity of the group to decide how time will be spent. Leader's attitudes and personal characteristics are far more important than the techniques that are used.	Leader is really not necessary at this stage if the group has been effective, for now the group is fairly self-directive and can draw on its own resources for direction. Leader may help the group members summarize what they have learned and encourage them to apply it to life outside the group.

Key techniques include active listening, reflection, clarification, self-disclosure, respect, congruence, and creation of a climate of trust. Members are encouraged to speak in an open way about whatever they are feeling at the moment. These tools do not represent techniques so much as basic attitudes/behaviors of the leader.

Questions to consider

Since active listening is a basis of this approach, ask yourself ways that your ability to hear and to understand might be hampered. What are some barriers in yourself to hearing others? Consider the following:

- talking too much and too soon

- being too concerned with answers, and not allowing members to explore feelings

- being too quick to give advice or to look for an easy solution

- asking too many closed questions

- being overly directive, and doing too much for the group

- selectively listening or looking for ways to confirm your preconceived notions about members

- paying too much attention to the content and to words, and failing to hear subtle meanings

Are you able to tolerate the expression of negative feelings within a group? Can you accept in a nondefensive manner negative feelings that are directed toward you?

Are you able and willing to share your own reactions in an appropriate manner with the members?

Do you avoid getting caught up in roles? Are you able to be yourself in the group, or do you hide behind professional roles?

Do you trust the members with your feelings? Are you able to let them know how they are affecting you?

How do you demonstrate respect for the members by your behavior in the group? Does your behavior indicate understanding and acceptance?

Are you able to facilitate a group rather than direct it? Can you let the members lead the way, helping them look at their process when necessary?

As a person and as a group facilitator, have you allowed yourself to be changed by a group? Are you open to growth yourself? What changes do you detect in yourself?

Are you able to be both supportive and confrontive? Can you provide nurturing and challenge at the same time?

Have you facilitated the group in such a manner that the members no longer look to you for direction or answers? Is the group able to function largely independently of you?

Reactions: Summarize your reactions to the person-centered perspective on group developmental stages. What do you like most? least? What aspects of this approach would you incorporate in your style of leadership?

ate empathy for others? What kind of person do you have a hard time empathizing with, and what does this tell you about yourself?

4. Unconditional positive regard and acceptance. What do the terms unconditional positive regard and acceptance mean to you? Rogers sees these as necessary qualities for therapeutic progress. Do you have these qualities? What prejudices or assumptions might you have that make it difficult for you to accept some people? Do you think that unconditional acceptance is desirable? Would you put certain conditions on your acceptance of people? If so, what might some of these conditions be?

5. Respect. What are some specific ways to demonstrate respect for group members? Do you think it's possible to work effectively with group members if you don't respect them? Why or why not? What are some common ways in which group leaders can show disrespect to members?

6. Genuineness. What criteria can you employ to determine your level of genuineness? Rogers contends that genuineness is essential for a therapeutic relationship to develop. Do you agree? Is it possible to be an effective group leader and not be genuine? What problems do you predict you might have in "being yourself" as a group leader?

7. Immediacy. Direct mutual talk conveys immediacy. Leaders can model this direct form of communication for members. What might get in your way of being direct? When is immediacy especially useful in a group?

8. Concreteness. Group members and leaders often speak in vague and general terms. How can you become more concrete in your own responses? How can you assist members to become more concrete in the ways they express their thoughts and feelings?

9. Confrontation. What is confrontation, as you see it? Does it occupy a central place in person-centered therapy? How can confrontation be combined with support? How can you challenge members without causing them to become increasingly defensive? What are your guidelines for using confrontation as a leader? What problems might you have that could make it difficult for you to confront members, even when it is needed?

10. Role and functions of the group leader. According to the person-centered view, the counselor in a group is more of a facilitator than a director, leader, teacher, or trainer. As a facilitator, you must create a psychological climate of safety and acceptance, which supposedly allows the members to use their own resources constructively. What do you think of this role? Could you function effectively in such a role? Why or why not?

11. Evaluation and research. Rogers stresses subjective research on group processes and outcomes, consisting mainly of self-reports by the participants. What do you think of subjective measures to determine the outcomes of a group? What are some of your ideas regarding ways of finding out whether a group is successful? How would you evaluate the outcome of your groups?

12. Critique of person-centered approach. Give your personal evaluation and critique of this model, using some of these questions as a guide:

- What would it be like for you to lead a group with a strict person-centered orientation?

- Do you think that techniques, knowledge of theory, and leadership skills are less important than the attitude of the counselor? Why or why not?

- Can you use many of the concepts and attitudes of this approach as a foundation for creating a therapeutic relationship and thus as a springboard to using other therapeutic techniques? If so, how?

- What are your major criticisms of this model?

- What are the major contributions of the person-centered model to group therapy?

- What ethical issues can you think of that might be raised by the person-centered approach to group work?

13. In the person-centered group there is very little advance planning and not much structuring on the facilitator's part. How do you think you'd function as a group leader without planning and without attempting to provide the group with a structure? If you were a member of such a group, how do you think you'd react to the lack of structure and planned activities by the facilitator?

14. What basic principles of the person-centered approach do you think are especially relevant to family therapy? What key concepts could you draw upon to facilitate open communication within a family group? How might a family be somewhat like and unlike any other small group?

11

GESTALT THERAPY

PRECHAPTER PRIMER AND SELF-INVENTORY FOR
GESTALT THERAPY

Directions: Refer to page 58 for general directions. Indicate your position on each statement, using the following code:

5 = I strongly agree with this statement.

4 = I agree, in most respects, with this statement.

3 = I am undecided in my opinion about this statement.

2 = I disagree, in most respects, with this statement.

1 = I strongly disagree with this statement.

_____ 1. The goal of group counseling is to help members integrate the fragmented parts of their personality enough that they can carry on the process of development alone.

_____ 2. Group work should focus on here-and-now experiencing in order to increase members' awareness.

_____ 3. Past conflicts or events are best understood by reexperiencing them in the here and now.

_____ 4. It is generally more productive to ask "what" and "how" questions than to ask "why" questions.

_____ 5. Unfinished business from the past tends to manifest itself in one's current behavior.

_____ 6. Group work should explore the members' nonverbal messages and blocks to awareness.

_____ 7. Fantasy is a potentially powerful therapeutic tool.

_____ 8. The most creative and effective experiments grow out of what is happening in the group.

_____ 9. The best way to deal with future concerns is to bring them into the here and now.

_____ 10. Exploration of group members' dreams is one of the leader's major methods of increasing members' awareness.

SUMMARY OF BASIC ASSUMPTIONS AND KEY CONCEPTS OF THE GESTALT APPROACH

1. The here and now of the group members' experience is most important. The group leader focuses on "what" and "how," instead of "why," and on anything that prevents effective functioning in the present.

2. People are personally responsible for what they feel.

3. Unfinished business from the past can interfere with effective functioning in the here and now. In order to remove this interference, group members should be encouraged to reexperience this business in the present.

4. The therapist should challenge group members to see how they are avoiding responsibility for their own feelings and encourage them to look for internal, rather than external, support.

5. Gestalt therapists use a wide range of action-oriented techniques in assisting group members to increase their awareness. Through group interaction, it is assumed, members will become more aware of conflicts and places where they "get stuck" (arrive at an impasse), and in the group they can experiment with a variety of techniques to work through the impasse and move to a new level of integration.

6. One of the group leader's tasks is to help clients locate the ways they are blocking energy and the ways their resistance is expressed in their body. Members can then be encouraged to try more adaptive behaviors.

7. The essence of creative therapy is designing experiments that grow out of the existential situation of the therapy encounter. The imaginative group invents experiments for itself that are tailor-made for what is happening in the moment.

STAGES OF DEVELOPMENT OF THE GESTALT GROUP

Dimension	Initial Stage	Working Stage	Final Stage
Key developmental tasks and goals	A central goal is to gain here-and-now awareness of what is being felt, sensed, and thought; group members must experiment and experience. Personal goals include achieving contact with self and others and defining one's boundaries with clarity.	Members deal with unfinished business from the past that is impeding full functioning now. The task is to integrate polarities. Group therapy is aimed at helping members give expression to the side of themselves that they tend to repress.	Members assume personal responsibility, which means that they integrate the fragmented aspects of their personalities. By achieving a moment-to-moment awareness of whatever is being experienced, members have within themselves the means to make changes.
Role of group leader and tasks	It is leader's task to follow whatever leads are provided by group members; in this way, members are able to become aware of the "what" and the "how" of their experiencing. Leader functions much like an artist by inventory techniques that arise from the material in the group. Leaders use themselves as persons in the group.	Leader's task is to pay close attention to both the verbal and nonverbal messages of members and to go with what is obvious. Focusing on the obvious makes therapy meaningful. Leader suggests experiments designed to enhance and intensify the experiences of the members. Leader pays attention to energy and helps members recognize their resistance.	After a piece of work is completed, leader may ask members to state how they are feeling. There is not much emphasis on cognitive structuring or behavior modification. It is assumed that, once members gain an awareness of what they are doing to prevent themselves from fully experiencing the moment, they are capable of changing.
Role of group members	Members are expected to focus on the here and now and to reexperience past conflicts as though they were going on now. Members decide what they will explore in the group. Members are challenged to accept responsibility for whatever they are experiencing and doing. They learn to live up to their own expectations, and they make decisions.	Members are expected to directly communicate to one another and to make "I" statements. They are discouraged from asking "why" questions and instead are urged to make personal statements. The focus is on exploration of feelings. To experience these feelings fully, members take part in a variety of action-oriented activities. They don't talk about problems, rather, they act out their various roles and conflicts.	Members give and receive feedback. They have the opportunity to identify unfinished business from their past that impedes present functioning and to work through impasses. By gaining awareness of areas that were out of awareness, they become more integrated. They are increasingly able to live with their own polarities.

Techniques	A wide range of experiential techniques all have the general goal of helping members intensify their experiencing in the present moment. Members may explore dreams by becoming all parts of their dreams; they may engage in role playing, in which they act out all the parts; or they may exaggerate a particular gesture or mannerism. Symbolic encounters are used to help members deal with unfinished situations.	Members can be asked to enact a situation the way they'd like it to be; they play all the parts. Members are often asked to give a new ending to an old and unfinished situation. Techniques help members see how past unfinished situations get in the way of effective living in the present. Members are asked to practice and experiment with new ways outside of the group. Action follows experiencing.
	Leader uses "what" and "how" questions, but not "why" questions, to help members focus on themselves and what they might be experiencing. Leaders may use many techniques, such as fantasy approaches, asking people to pay attention to what they are experiencing physically, thinking out loud, and so on. The skilled leader avoids grabbing techniques from a bag. Rather, leader creates experiments that express what is going on in the group now.	
Questions to consider	Are you able to create a climate within the group that encourages members to try out creative experiments? Have you prepared them for Gestalt techniques? Have you earned their respect and trust? Do they see benefits in participating in a variety of experiments aimed at enhancing their awareness?	How can you create experiments that will help members gain awareness of what they are doing to prevent themselves from being fully in the present?
	Do you avoid using planned techniques to make something happen in a group? Can you follow the process and invent a technique that will highlight members' concerns?	How can members be helped to work through unfinished business from their past that interferes with living now in a vital way? How can any unfinished business within the group be addressed at the final stage?
	Do you take care to avoid being mechanical in using techniques? Are the methods you employ an extension of the person you are?	Have the members recognized ways that they block their strengths and keep themselves from living the way they want?
	Do you invite members to take part in an experiment, as opposed to commanding them?	Are you able to help members deal with their feelings about termination? Do you encourage them to express feelings about separation?
	Can you respect resistance in a group member? Are you able to work therapeutically with resistance?	
	Do you focus on what is going on within the group now? Are you able to pay attention to the subtle nonverbal messages and work with them?	
	Do you help members stay with their present experience and not talk about what they are thinking or feeling?	
	Do you bring yourself in as a person, and do you respond to others in personal ways?	

Reactions: Summarize your reactions to the Gestalt perspective on group developmental stages. What do you like most? least? What aspect of this approach would you incorporate in your style of leadership?

EXERCISES AND ACTIVITIES FOR GESTALT GROUPS

Rationale

Gestalt therapy makes use of a variety of action-oriented techniques that are designed to intensify what members are experiencing. Instead of discussing conflicts, for example, members are encouraged to "become the conflict." The idea is to fully experience every dimension of oneself (be authentic). The Gestaltist contends that, when we get close to feelings that make us uncomfortable, we tend to avoid these feelings and thus do not really fully experience the various dimensions of a conflict. The Gestalt therapist will suggest experiments to help members try some new behavior and thus experience everything fully.

It is important that the following exercises <u>not</u> be done mechanically. Each exercise is best if it is tailored to the unique needs of the members in your class/group. Further, it is a good idea to give members some preparation before springing an experiment on them. Enlist the cooperation of group members by giving brief explanations of the basic purpose of each exercise. By trying many of the exercises in your own small group, you will be in a better position to know which of these techniques you might want to use when you are a group leader.

Exercises

1. <u>Here and now versus there and then.</u> Talk about a personal experience in the past tense for about three minutes. Then, relive the same experience as though it were happening in the present. What difference do you notice between these three-minute exercises? What value do you see in encouraging people in groups to make past experiences into present-centered ones?

2. <u>Bringing the future into the now.</u> Are you anticipating any future confrontations? This exercise can be a form of rehearsal. Using the two-chair technique, be yourself, then become the person you expect to confront, then be yourself, and so on. Make this future event happen in the here and now. Do so briefly. When you are finished, discuss what this experience was like. What did you learn through the experiment? What are your fears and hopes regarding this future event?

3. <u>How do you accept and avoid personal responsibility?</u> Using either a go-around approach, subgroups, or dyads, have each member say how he or she avoids accepting responsibility for his or her own thoughts, actions, feelings, and moods. How can you begin to accept more of the responsibility for the ways you blame others for your emotional states? Examples: "You <u>make</u> me mad." "You <u>get me</u> jealous." "You <u>keep me</u> from doing what I really want to do."

4. <u>Identifying unfinished business.</u> Gestalt therapy emphasizes the role of old business that hangs around and gets in the way of our being effective and alive now. In your group mention, without discussing them, one or two areas or specific examples of unfinished business. Then, you might add how you could work toward dealing with these unfinished themes. Some examples of unfinished business are:

- feeling stuck with guilt
- feeling resentful, and not expressing the resentment
- experiencing grief that has not been fully expressed

5. <u>Avoidance</u>. The concept of avoidance is central in Gestalt therapy. How many ways can you think of that you avoid things? Do you reach an impasse because you are afraid of feeling uncomfortable? Do you avoid giving up games because you are afraid of what life would be like without them? Do you avoid changing by convincing yourself that you cannot change? Do you avoid by trying to convince yourself that you are perfectly satisfied? Do you avoid by blaming others? Try living out some of these avoidance techniques in your group. For example, really blame others for your ability to change.

6. <u>Language approaches</u>. In order to see how language can be used to alienate us from ourselves as well as others, deliberately try to use language as impersonally as you can. Conduct a short conversation using language that keeps you from being responsible for yourself and that is designed to alienate others. Here are some guidelines to a distant and impersonal language style.

- Say <u>it</u> instead of <u>I</u>.
- Use <u>you</u> when you are really talking about yourself, and avoid making "I" statements.
- Ask questions. Try pelleting others with questions for a few moments— interrogate, ask a lot of "why" questions, and take care to keep yourself out of any interchange.
- Use plenty of qualifiers; that is, either before you say anything or at the end of any sentence use a qualifier or a disclaimer, such as <u>but</u>, <u>maybe</u>, <u>sort of</u>, <u>kind of</u>, <u>perhaps</u>, <u>possibly</u>, <u>I guess</u>, <u>I suppose</u>, and so on.
- Say <u>can't</u> a lot (even if you know you can); saying <u>can't</u> will cement your feelings of helplessness.
- Pepper your talks with a good dose of <u>shoulds</u> and <u>oughts</u>. Be sure to tell others what they <u>should</u> do, how they <u>should</u> feel, what they <u>should</u> think; and tell them how they <u>ought</u> to be and <u>ought</u> not to be.

Talk about how it feels to talk this way, and get feedback from the group members on how they experienced your doing this.

7. <u>Nonverbal language in group</u>. Exaggerate some of your typical body language. If you often frown, let yourself really get into that frown. If you have a certain mannerism, develop it fully. What can you learn from this exercise about your nonverbal language? Pay attention to others as they speak for a time, and note the tone of voice, the manner of speech, the quality of voice, the posture, facial expressions, gestures, the speed and rate of speech, and so on. What do people tell you about themselves nonverbally? Finally, each person in your group might try "becoming" one aspect of his or her body language. For example, Marilyn could "become" her tight mouth and then speak "for" her mouth: "I am my tightness, I'm holding my words back from you. I'm not going to be open, and if you want something from me you'll have to pry me open."

8. <u>Experimenting with dialogues</u>. Each person in the group at some time might want to experiment with the dialogue game. You can also do this at home alone. Simply put two chairs facing each other. Next, choose one of your conflicts; become one side of this conflict, and talk to the other side, which is in the other chair. Get up and sit in the other chair, becoming that other side. Carry on this dialogue for a time. If you're doing this in a group, discuss what you learned. What is it like for you to do the experiment? Which side felt dominant? Here are some examples of typical conflicts that often keep us fragmented:

- Part of me wants to open up; the other part of me wants to keep closed.

- There is the serious side of me, and then there is the fun side.

- I want to love, yet I don't dare let myself.

- Part of me wants to risk; the other part wants to play it safe.

List as many types of conflicts/fragmentations that exist inside of you as you can. Do you have trouble integrating dichotomies such as tough/tender, masculine/feminine, worthwhile/worthless?

9. <u>Fantasy approaches</u>. Try some fantasy experiments in the group. For instance, allow yourself to live out some of your expectations and fears. If you are afraid of being rejected, live out your rejection fantasies in your group. You can also use the rehearsal technique; as you think of your fantasy, repeat all your thoughts out loud.

10. <u>Gestalt dream work</u>. Try some Gestalt dream experiments in your group. For example, become all the parts of a dream—act them out in the present tense, and let yourself really experience the dream. Or carry on a dialogue between various parts of the dream. What does your dream teach you about yourself?

11. <u>Making the rounds.</u> In this exercise a member goes around to everyone in the group and says something to each person—usually something that he or she is attempting to deny, something that is difficult to say, or something that he or she typically does not express. Make up some incomplete sentences, and experiment with making the rounds and completing these sentences. Some examples of incomplete sentences are:

- "If I were to depend on you, then _____."

- "I keep my distance from you by _____."

- "If I were to get close to you, then _____."

- "If I'm not always in control, _____."

- "One way I'd try to control you is _____."

- "If I would not smile when I'm in pain, I _____."

- "When I look at you, _____."

Any of these sentences can be selected and completed for every person in the room. It is important that you respond quickly and give your uncensored and initial reaction. After you've experienced a go-around, it would be useful to talk about what you learned from it, what it was like for you to do this, and where you could go from here. You can also experiment with making concise statements to each person in the group, using the go-around method. For example, if you find it difficult to ask for anything for yourself, you could go to each person and ask for something.

12. Rehearsal. Internal rehearsal saps much of our vitality. We often think carefully about the appropriate way to be, so that any spontaneity is squelched. The rehearsal technique consists of saying out loud what you are thinking silently. In this exercise, select a situation in which you would typically rehash all the pros and cons to yourself before deciding what to do or say—but this time allow yourself to think out loud. In your rehearsal, let yourself ham it up a bit and really get the feel of the exercise. For example, let yourself act out in a group what you go through before you ask a person for a date. What are all the things you say to yourself? (The exercise can make you more acutely aware of how you are striving for approval or how much you fear rejection.)

13. Reversal techniques. In this procedure, you give expression to a side of yourself that rarely gets expressed. Gestalt theory posits that each person's polarities crave expression yet are often not acknowledged, much less directly expressed. For example, the very prim and proper lady in the group who continually worries about the appropriateness of her performances can be invited to experiment with deliberately inappropriate behavior. She is given permission to be unladylike. The rationale here is that integration of polarities is possible if you allow yourself to plunge into the very thing that produces anxiety in you.

14. The secret. This exercise can be useful in exploring fears, guilt feelings, and catastrophic expectations. Think of a personal secret. Don't actually share the secret in the group, but imagine yourself doing so. What do you imagine it would be like if others knew your secret? What are your fears? How do you imagine they'd respond? (If you'd like, you can discuss these fears or your fantasy experience in the group.)

15. The projection exercise. At times, people accuse others of the very things that they refuse to see in themselves. For example, you may see others as being critical and judgmental of you while failing to experience how you are very critical and judgmental of others. In this exercise you make a direct statement to others in the group and then apply it to yourself. For instance, you might say to Al "You continually expect me to be more than I am in here." Then turn it around and say "Al, I expect more from you in this group." Try a new statement with each person, and apply all of these sentences to yourself. What can you learn from this exercise?

16. Review all of the preceding exercises, and decide what techniques you might use in working with the following conflicts:

   • trust versus mistrust

   • the desire to get close and the need to pull away

   • being weak versus being strong

- the will to risk <u>and</u> the need to play it safe

- being appropriate versus being inappropriate

- love <u>and</u> hate

- the wish to express anger <u>and</u> the fear of doing so

- dependence versus independence

- wanting to disclose yourself <u>and</u> wanting to remain secretive

Can you think of other conflicts or problems whose solutions might be aided by the use of the Gestalt-therapy techniques you have learned about in these exercises?

QUESTIONS FOR DISCUSSION AND EVALUATION

1. Gestalt therapy is an action-oriented approach, one that requires the group leader to be active and employ a variety of experiments designed to enable members to intensify their feelings. How comfortable are you in using such an approach? What is your opinion of the therapeutic value of these Gestalt experiments? How do you imagine you would respond to these techniques as a group member?

2. Techniques cannot be separated from the personality of the leader and the relationship he or she has with the group members. Do you see the danger of a group leader's becoming a mere technician and keeping him- or herself hidden through the use of techniques? If you are practicing Gestalt therapy, how can you avoid merely employing one gimmick after another? Would you, as a leader, tend to use these techniques as a way to get power? Discuss the potential for abuse of power by the group leader.

3. How can a therapist combine the Gestalt approach with other approaches, such as psychodrama, transactional analysis, and rational-emotive therapy? What kind of integration do you see with other systems?

4. How do you deal with members who don't want to (or are afraid to) participate in a Gestalt experiment. If you were to invite a member to try out some new behavior and the member refused, what do you imagine you might say?

5. What psychological risks do you see as being involved in a Gestalt group? How would you prepare members for taking part in Gestalt experiments? What safeguards can you think of that might lessen the potential dangers of Gestalt techniques?

6. What difference do you see between using preplanned techniques in a group and inventing experiments that grow out of what is happening in the group situation?

7. In general, what is the rationale of most of the Gestalt techniques described in this chapter? As a leader, what would you be trying to accomplish by using many of these experiments? Can you think of some ways

that you might explain this rationale to members who are not familiar with Gestalt procedures?

8. What uses can you see in working in a Gestalt manner with dreams in a group setting? What are some ways you can think of to link one member's dream work with other members?

9. Some Gestalt therapists prefer to work on an intrapsychic level. They focus on one person for a time as other members observe the work of that individual. Other Gestalt leaders tend to focus on interpersonal dynamics, and they make attempts to increase active contact between participants. In the latter style of leadership there is a clear focus on group process, and the social interactional nature of an individual's work is fully explored. What advantages and disadvantages do you see in each of these styles of leadership? Which style do you prefer?

10. What concepts and techniques of Gestalt therapy do you think are particularly useful in working with families? If you were doing family therapy, what possibilities would you see in applying Gestalt procedures? How might you work differently with an intact family group than with any other group?

12

TRANSACTIONAL ANALYSIS

PRECHAPTER PRIMER AND SELF-INVENTORY
FOR THE TA APPROACH

Directions: Refer to page 58 for general directions. Indicate your position on these statements, using the following code:

5 = I strongly agree with this statement.

4 = I agree, in most respects, with this statement.

3 = I am undecided in my opinion about this statement.

2 = I disagree, in most respects, with this statement.

1 = I strongly disagree with this statement.

_____ 1. For healthy personality development, positive stroking (physical and emotional touching) is essential.

_____ 2. Group leaders should play the roles of teacher, trainer, and resource person.

_____ 3. Contracts are both basic and necessary if the group-counseling process is to be therapeutic.

_____ 4. Group members should develop independence and not rely on the group leader for guidance.

_____ 5. Relationships between the group leader and members must be equal if the group's work is to be successful.

_____ 6. Group members should be taught how to explore the early decisions and parental injunctions that influence them now.

_____ 7. Group members should be taught to examine the decisions they made early in life and determine if these decisions are still appropriate.

_____ 8. Game playing, by its very definition, prevents the development of genuine intimacy.

_____ 9. People tend to accept uncritically the messages they received from their parents and from parental substitutes.

_____ 10. Contracts give direction to group sessions, increase the responsibility of members to actively participate in group work, and provide a basis for equal partnership between the members and the leader.

SUMMARY OF BASIC ASSUMPTIONS AND KEY CONCEPTS
OF THE TA APPROACH

1. People make necessary decisions early in life that may later become inappropriate.

2. In order to make new, appropriate decisions, group members are taught to recognize ego states, to understand how injunctions and messages they incorporated as children affect them now, and to identify life scripts that determine their actions.

3. TA, then, is largely a didactic and cognitive form of therapy, with the goal of liberating group members from the past and assisting them to redecide how they will live based on new awareness.

4. Group members can best achieve these goals by being active in the group-therapy process, and thus TA group therapists stress the equality of the therapeutic relationship between group members and therapists.

5. To assure that members actively and responsibly participate in the group-therapy process, they contract to work on specific issues, and these contracts direct the course of the group.

6. TA concepts and techniques are particularly appropriate for group work. It is in a group context that people best learn how they interact with one another, how decisions made early in life still influence them, and how to become aware of the games they play and the scripts they live out.

STAGES IN THE DEVELOPMENT OF THE TA GROUP

Dimension	Initial Stage	Working Stage	Final Stage
Key developmental tasks and goals	Group therapy begins with a contract, one that is acceptable to both member and leader. Group work is guided by the contract. An early basic task is to teach members the basics of TA, including how to recognize ego states, transactions, games, injunctions, rackets, and the significance of early decisions.	At the working stage, the basic developmental task is that members recognize and work through impasses. Much work is done with re-experiencing early decisions and situations from childhood, with the aim of making new decisions that are more appropriate for the present. Early decisions are reviewed critically, and members think about ways they want to be different.	Focus at this stage is on actually making new decisions. Basic premise is that what was decided earlier can now be redecided. Members learn to thrive on positive strokes, and they recognize the power they possess. Contracts may be renegotiated, and new work may begin.
Role of group leader and tasks	Leaders begin to teach members that they are responsible for how they act, think, and feel. Leaders provide structure for the group, teach the basic concepts of TA, and may use role-playing and fantasy methods to have members relive certain scenes. Leaders help members identify and clarify goals and develop a contract that will specify the work to be done.	At this stage the group leader assists members to recognize early decisions they made from a Child ego state, and then, from this same ego state, the members are encouraged to make new and more appropriate decisions. Leaders draw on a variety of techniques to help members work through impasses.	At the final stage of a group, the leaders mainly assist members in making new decisions and life-oriented contracts; members are encouraged to accept responsibility for changing their own life.
Role of group members	Members are expected to formulate a clear contract. They learn the ego state they are functioning in, recognize the injunctions they've accepted, and see the importance of understanding and challenging early decisions.	Members learn about the injunction/decision/racket complex. They identify life scripts. Members work through early experiences both cognitively and affectively.	During the final stage, the members decide how they will change. They may use the group to practice new behaviors. Feedback and support are given.

Techniques	Contracts are a basic tool. Imagery and fantasy techniques may be used. Role playing may be used to promote a here-and-now focus. The other techniques TA leaders tend to use are life-script analysis and working with injunctions and decisions.	A wide range of cognitive and affective techniques is used, including structural analysis, transactional analysis, analysis of games, cognitive restructuring, empty-chair, life-script questionnaire, desensitization. Techniques in TA groups are designed to help members feel more intensely and to think and conceptualize.	Homework assignments may be used as a way of helping the members to fulfill their contracts. Gestalt techniques may be incorporated into the TA group, as may techniques drawn from behavioral methods, psychodrama, and other action-oriented approaches.
Questions to consider	Are you able to obtain a clear and specific contract from each of the members? How can you help members formulate a therapeutic contract? Are these contracts open to renegotiation? Are the members committed to working on them? How does the structure of the group reflect the nature of the members' contracts? What would you most want to teach the members about how a TA group functions? What is your role as leader in this group? What do you expect from the members? What kind of structuring do you most want to provide? To what degree have you explored your own injunctions and early decisions? How might this influence the way you lead your group?	What kind of information would you want to include in a life-script questionnaire? How might you use this life-script checklist in your TA group? What are some techniques for focusing on injunctions and early decisions? How can you become aware of members' games, life positions, and life scripts by paying attention to their transactions with others in the sessions? How might you draw upon techniques from Gestalt therapy, psychodrama, and behavior therapy in working with concepts in the TA framework? What are some ways you might help members work through early experiences that have an impact on their present behavior?	To what degree have the members recognized early decisions and the life-script they have been living by, and to what extent are they making new decisions? Are they acting on these redecisions in the group? Are they taking action outside of the sessions? What new contracts might you make with members as a group approaches the final stage? How can you teach members to find support outside of the group for maintaining the changes? What are some ways to reinforce redecisions by the client and by others in the group. What are some ways to prepare members for some new situations that they will face when they leave the group? How about preparing them for dealing with setbacks?

Reactions: Summarize your reactions to the TA perspective on group developmental stages. What do you like most? least? What aspects of this approach would you incorporate in your style of leadership?

EXERCISES AND ACTIVITIES FOR THE TA APPROACH

Rationale

Not all of the following exercises deal with therapeutic procedures routinely used by all TA practitioners; however, they are designed to increase your awareness of matters such as these: What ego state do you tend to function in? What kind of strokes do you typically receive? Which of the parental messages that you picked up early in life do you still live by? How do your decisions made early in life still influence you? What games prevent intimacy? What is the basis for new decisions?

Many of these exercises are cognitively oriented and are geared to get you to think about your assumptions and your behavior. I encourage you to think of imaginative ways of developing your own exercises; for example, experiment with combining some of these cognitively oriented TA concepts with some of the emotion-oriented techniques of Gestalt therapy. Use these exercises in your own small groups, and discuss specific aspects of this approach that you think you could use in the groups you lead.

Exercises

1. The ego states: Parent, Adult, Child. TA teaches people in groups to recognize when they are operating in their Parent, Adult, and Child ego states. Each person in your group should choose an ego state and remain in it during a group exercise. Each person should think and speak from the chosen ego state. The purpose of this exercise is to help you become aware of how you might function as a Parent without knowing it. As a variation, you might try having two group members conduct a debate between two ego states.

2. Stroking. TA stresses the need for strokes, both physical and psychological ones. In your group, talk about the specific types of stroke that you need to sustain you. What strokes do you seek? How do you get the strokes you want? Are you able to accept positive stroking, or do you have a need to discount it and set yourself up for negative stroking? You could also experiment with asking your group members for the strokes you want. Discuss in your group the idea of conditional strokes. Were you brought up to believe that you would get strokes when you behaved in the expected manner? How does this relate to the strokes you get in your group?

3. Injunctions. Injunctions are messages that we have been programmed to accept—that is, messages that we have knowingly and unknowingly incorporated into our life-style. In this experiment, each group member "becomes" his or her parent and gives injunctions. Each person should adopt the tone of voice that he or she imagines the parent would have used. Get involved in the exercise, and really tell people the way you think they should be and should live. As a second part of this exercise you might discuss a few of the following injunctions as they apply to you. What are some other messages that you heard as a child? Add these to the list. Which of these messages still influence you?

- Don't be _____.

- You should always do what is expected.

- Don't feel/think/be who you are.

- Don't succeed/fail.

- Don't trust others.

- Be perfect—never make a mistake.

- Be more than you are.

- Don't be impulsive.

- Don't be sexy.

- Don't be aggressive.

- Keep your feelings to yourself.

- You ought to think of others before yourself.

- You should never have negative thoughts.

Which of these injunctions have you accepted uncritically? Which of them do you most want to modify?

4. <u>Decisions and redecisions</u>. People tend to cling to early decisions and look for evidence to support these decisions. However, TA assumes that what has been decided can be redecided. In your group, devote some time to identifying your early decisions. Then, determine what you are doing to keep them current. Finally, discuss what you might do to change these archaic decisions so that you are not held back by them. For example, you may have decided early on to keep all of your negative feelings inside you, for you had been told both directly and indirectly that you were unacceptable when you expressed negative feelings. In this case, you could discuss what you do now in situations where you experience negative feelings. Do you feel that you want to change your old decision?

5. <u>Exploring your rackets</u>. In TA, a "racket" refers to the collection of bad feelings that people use to justify their life script and the feelings on which they base their decisions. Some possible rackets are:

- an anger racket

- a guilt racket

- a hurt racket

- a depression racket

For instance, if you develop a depression racket, you may actually seek out situations that will support your feelings of depression. You will continually do things to make yourself feel depressed, and thus you will feel this way enough of the time to be able to convince yourself that you are right to have these feelings. In your group, spend some time exploring how you maintain old, chronic, bad feelings. What might be one of your major rackets? List some recent situations that you put yourself

109

in or found yourself in that led to old, familiar feelings of depression, guilt, or the like.

6. <u>Games we play</u>. In this group exercise, devote some time to listing some of the games that you played as a child to get what you wanted. For example, perhaps you played the Helplessness Game. If you act helpless and pretend you cannot do something, then others may treat you as helpless and do for you what you really don't want to do for yourself. Thus, if you did not want to make your own decisions as a child for fear of the consequences, you played stupid, and your parents then did for you what you were unwilling to do for yourself. True, you did get something from the game, but how does the price you paid compare with what you got? In your group, discuss some games you played as a child, then list what you got from each game and the price you paid for the gains. What games do you play now? Discuss what you get from these games. Evaluate the costs. What do you think you'd be like if you gave up these games?

7. <u>Life positions</u>. Have each person in your group briefly describe himself or herself with respect to self-esteem. Do you genuinely like and appreciate yourself? Can you feel like a winner without putting another person down? Do you think you are right and the rest of the world is wrong? Or do you continually put yourself down? Early in life you might have felt that everyone around you was just fine and that you were basically rotten to the core. What are some of the situations that led to these feelings of inadequacy? How might you challenge these feelings now? Would you classify yourself as a winner or a loser?

8. <u>Changes in your life circumstances</u>. You may have felt basically inadequate as a child, yet now you may feel very adequate in many areas of your life. What factors do you think are responsible for this shift in the way you feel about yourself?

9. <u>A book of you</u>. Write your own table of contents for a book about your life, and then give your book a title, What title best captures the sense of your life now? What would you include in the chapters? Mention the key turning points and key events of your life in your table of contents, so that others in your group will have a picture of who you are. Now, assume you want to revise your book. What revisions do you want to make, chapter by chapter? Do you want a new book title?

10. <u>"You are your parents" exercise</u>. This exercise can be done with a partner or in small groups. It will provide a format for looking at the influence your parents have on you and the quality of life you see your parents experiencing, and it will help you decide how you'd like to modify your own values and behavior. Close your eyes and see your parents at their present ages in a typical setting. Visualize the way they live. How is their marriage? How do they react to their children? What kind of life do they have? Now imagine yourself at their ages in the same setting. For a few minutes imagine that you value what they do and that your life is almost identical with theirs. In what ways would you modify the outcomes of this fantasy?

11. <u>Early decisions</u>. Assume that you are a group leader and that you determine that certain members have made the following decisions. Speculate about what factors may have contributed to each of these decisions:

- I'll always be a failure.

- I'm basically weak and helpless.

- I won't feel, and that way I won't experience pain.

- Regardless of what I accomplish, I'll never be good enough.

12. <u>Redecision work in groups</u>. Take the four statements above, and assume that each of them represents a life orientation. How would you proceed in working with each of these approaches toward life? What new decisions would you like to see made? What would it take to change these decisions?

13. <u>Contracts</u>. TA groups work on a contract basis, which means that members clearly specify what they want to change as well as what they are willing to <u>do</u> to change. What do you think of the use of contracts in groups? If you were to become involved as a client in a TA group, what are some contracts that you'd be willing to make? List one such contract, including a <u>specific</u> statement of some behavior you want to change and the steps you'd be willing to take to make this change.

14. <u>Personal Critique</u>. What is your personal evaluation of the TA approach to group work? Consider questions such as the following in your critique:

- To what clients do you think TA is best suited?

- What contributions of TA do you think are most significant?

- What are the major limitations of TA? Explain.

13

BEHAVIOR THERAPY

PRECHAPTER PRIMER AND SELF-INVENTORY FOR
THE BEHAVIORAL APPROACH

Directions: Refer to page 58 for general directions. Indicate your position on these statements, using the following code:

5 = I strongly agree with this statement.

4 = I agree, in most respects, with this statement.

3 = I am undecided in my opinion about this statement.

2 = I disagree, in most respects, with this statement.

1 = I strongly disagree with this statement.

_____ 1. Self-reinforcement is needed if participants hope to translate the changes made in a group to everyday life.

_____ 2. Assessment is a necessary step in the initial phase of a group.

_____ 3. Evaluation of results is best done continually during all the phases of a group.

_____ 4. For change to occur, members must actively participate in group work, and they must be willing to practice outside of group sessions.

_____ 5. Specificity in goal formation increases the chances that members will do productive group work.

_____ 6. Two of the group leader's functions are to provide reinforcement and to serve as a model.

_____ 7. Groups should aim at helping participants develop specific skills and self-directed methods of changing.

_____ 8. The group leader's attention to and interest in members serve as powerful sources of reinforcement.

_____ 9. Group members should decide on their own therapeutic goals.

_____ 10. Any group techniques or therapeutic procedures should be evaluated both by the group members and the leader to determine their effectiveness in meeting goals.

SUMMARY OF BASIC ASSUMPTIONS AND KEY CONCEPTS OF BEHAVIOR THERAPY

1. The essential characteristics of behavior therapy in groups are as follows: the target behaviors to be changed are specified; the observable events in the environment that maintain behavior are studied; the environmental changes and the intervention techniques that can modify behavior are specified; data-based assessment is a part of the treatment procedure; and there is a focus on transferring new skills learned in the group to everyday situations.

2. The behaviors that clients express are considered to be the problem (rather than merely symptoms of the problem).

3. A basic assumption is that all problematic behaviors, cognitions, and emotions have been learned and that they can be modified by new learning. Group therapy is seen as a teaching/learning process whereby clients are encouraged to try out more effective ways of changing their behaviors, cognitions, and emotions.

4. The group therapist is active and directive, functioning in some ways as a trainer or teacher. All the techniques used by the group therapist are based on principles of learning and geared toward behavior change. Diagnosis, testing, and data gathering are frequently used. The therapist is not interested in the client's past, unconscious material, or other internal states; rather, he or she focuses on manipulating environmental variables.

5. The members must actively participate in the group work and be willing to experiment with new behavior by taking a role in bringing about changes in behavior.

STAGES IN THE DEVELOPMENT OF THE BEHAVIORAL THERAPY GROUP

Dimension	Initial Stage	Working Stage	Final Stage
Key developmental tasks and goals	Responsibilities and expectations of both the leaders and the members are outlined in a contract. Preparation of members is stressed. At the early stages, focus is on building cohesion, getting familiar with the structure of group therapy, and identifying problems to explore. Assessment is a vital aspect, as is setting of clear goals. A treatment plan, including procedures to be used to attain the stated goals, is developed and is constantly evaluated to test its effectiveness.	Treatment plan is implemented. A wide range of treatment procedures is used to solve specific problems, and focus is on learning new skills. Central part of this phase is work done outside of the group. The group is used as a place to learn and perfect new skills and to gain support and feedback so that progress continues. Much of the learning in the group takes place through modeling and observation, along with coaching. The emphasis is on behavior (changing unadaptive behavior or learning new skills) as opposed to the exploration of feelings.	At this phase the transfer of learning from the group to everyday life is critical. Situations that simulate the real world are used, so that this transfer is facilitated. Focus is on learning self-directed behavior and developing plans for maintaining and using new coping skills. It is assumed that the generalization of learning will not occur by chance, so sessions are structured in such a manner that transfer of learning will be maximized.
Role of group leader and tasks	Leaders' tasks are to conduct pre-group interviews and screen members, organize the group, prepare the members by telling them how the group will work, establish group trust and cohesion, assess the nature of the problems to be explored, and provide a structure for the group. Leaders are active, and they provide information. They assist members in formulating specific goals.	Leaders develop an appropriate treatment plan based on the initial assessment, and they monitor those behaviors identified as problematic. They continually assess progress and teach the members self-evaluation skills. Leaders reinforce desired behavior, and they assist members in learning methods of self-reinforcement. Leaders serve the function of modeling, coaching, and providing corrective feedback.	Main function of leader at this phase is to assist members in learning ways to transfer new skills acquired in the group to situations in daily life. Leader prepares members for dealing with setbacks and teaches them skills needed to meet new situations effectively. Leader arranges for follow-up interviews to assess the impact of the group and to determine the degree to which members have fulfilled their contracts.
Role of group members	Members are involved in formulating the contract. They make a list of behaviors they want to change, or they clarify the problems that they want to work on in the group. They determine baseline data for certain behaviors and begin to monitor and to observe their behavior in the group as well. The members are in-	Members report on the nature of their progress each week. Group time is used to define problem areas to work on in the group. Role playing of a behavioral nature is done to assist members in learning new skills. Members provide models for one another; they must carry out specific behavioral assign-	Members decide what specific things they've learned in the group situation, and they practice new roles and behaviors, both in the group and in daily life. Feedback is provided so that skills and new behaviors can be refined, and suggestions are made for maintaining these new behavioral changes.

	volved in the assessment process, which continues throughout the group.	ments, keep records of their progress, assess their progress in light of the baseline data collected at the initial sessions, and report to the group each week.	Members act as a support system for one another. They typically agree to carry out specific assignments at the end of a group and then report back at a follow-up meeting.
Techniques	Basic techniques include contracts, checklists, role playing, and assessment devices.	Many behavioral techniques are used, including reinforcement, modeling, desensitization, cognitive methods, and homework assignments.	Feedback is a main technique, as is role playing and developing self-reinforcement systems. Follow-up sessions are scheduled to assess outcomes.
Questions to consider	Central function of leader is to create trust needed for work on issues. In doing this, leader must strive to make the group attractive to members, create many functional roles that they can play in the group, and find ways to involve all members in the group interactions. How can you best carry out these tasks? How can you help the members develop specific and concrete goals? Are the goals that are established meaningful for the members? Have they been developed by the members and the leader in a spirit of cooperation? What are specific things you expect of members?	What are the ways that you will assist members in the process of assessment, monitoring, and evaluation throughout the working stage? How might you involve the members in developing a treatment plan for a group? What kind of structuring would you want to provide in a behavioral group? What specific behaviors would you most want to reinforce in members? What are some ways that you might involve other members in one person's work? How could you use members to provide assistance to one another between sessions? What ways could you think of to use a buddy system?	How can you change your role from that of a direct therapist to a consultant during the final stage? How can you encourage the members to assume an increasing share of the leadership tasks? What self-help skills and problem-solving strategies would you want to teach members as a group is approaching termination? What kinds of short-term and long-term follow-up session might you consider setting up before a group ends? Along with members, how can you evaluate the effectiveness of a given group?

Reactions: Summarize your reactions to the behavioral perspective on group developmental stages. What do you like most? least? What aspects of this approach would you incorporate in your leadership style?

EXERCISES AND ACTIVITIES FOR THE
BEHAVIORAL APPROACH

Rationale

Behaviorally oriented group leaders use a variety of specific techniques. These research-based techniques are used systematically to accomplish particular goals, and ongoing assessment is made by both the group members and the leader to determine whether these methods are producing positive results. If members are not making progress, then the therapeutic procedures can be modified. It is basic to the behavioral approach that therapeutic procedures and evaluation of these techniques proceed simultaneously.

Most of the behavioral techniques are designed to effect specific behavioral changes—that is, either to decrease or eliminate undesirable behaviors or to acquire or increase desired behaviors. The following exercises will show you ways to apply learning principles in your work to change behavior. You can apply many of the techniques presented in these exercises to your own life. As you experiment with these techniques in your small groups or in class, determine which aspects of the behavioral approach you could incorporate in your work as a group leader, regardless of the theoretical model you might be working with.

Exercises

1. Setting up a behavioral group. Assume that you are a behaviorally oriented group leader and are giving a talk to a community gathering where you hope to begin a group. What points would you emphasize to give these people a good picture of your group, your functions and role as a leader, and the things that would be expected of them as participants? Assume that they respond enthusiastically and want to join your group. Where would you begin, and how would you proceed in setting up this group? What pregroup concerns would you have? What would you do during the initial meeting?

2. Terminating and evaluating a group. Assume that the above group meets for 20 weeks. It is now the 18th week. What would you be concerned with as a group leader? Mention specific issues that you'd want the group to deal with. What evaluation procedures would you employ at the end of the group? What follow-up procedures would you use?

3. Relaxation exercises. Many behavioral group therapists use self-relaxation techniques; members are taught how to systematically relax every part of their body. They practice this in the group and also at home on a daily basis. In your own group, one of you can volunteer to lead a relaxation exercise using the tension-relaxation procedure, going from head to foot. After the exercise, discuss the possibilities for using relaxation procedures in any group. What are the values of such procedures? Consider practicing these exercises to reduce unnecessary stress. Give them at least a three-week trial to determine some personal benefits.

4. Behavioral family therapy. Assume that you are to counsel a family as a group. What techniques might you use that are behavioral in nature? Think of ways that you could apply what you read in this chapter to facilitating family-therapy sessions. What are some examples of behavioral homework assignments that you can ask family members to practice as an adjunct to the group sessions?

5. Social reinforcement. Observe in your own class or group how social reinforcement works. For example, for what are members reinforced? Pay attention to nonverbal responses, such as smiles, head nodding, and body posture, as well as verbal support and approval. Do you see ways that you can systematically use social reinforcement in a group situation? What social reinforcers have the most impact on your behavior? Support? compliments? applause?

6. Modeling. It is important for you to realize that, as a group leader, you continually model behaviors for the members. What behaviors would you most want to model? Some that you might consider are clear and direct speech, self-disclosure, respect, enthusiasm, sensitivity, and caring confrontation. In your group, discuss ways that you can model positive behavior. Also, observe the effect of a certain behavior on your group (for example, speaking enthusiastically). Do you notice that members tend to assume some of the traits of the leader? What are the implications of this?

7. Assertion-training groups: an introduction. Assume that you are giving a talk to people who might be interested in joining the assertion-training group that you are forming. What would you tell them about your group? What is assertive behavior? Whom is the group for? How can it help them? What would they do in this group? What are some of the techniques that you'd use during the group sessions? For this exercise, two of those in your group can be the co-leaders and explain all about the group to the potential members; the others in the group can ask questions relating to what they will be expected to do in the group, how this will help them in daily life, and how they can apply what they learn.

8. Applying assertive-training procedures to yourself. In an exercise related to the preceding one, think of an area where you have difficulty being assertive. This may involve dealing with supervisors, returning faulty merchandise, or expressing positive feelings. In your own group, you can experiment with improving your assertiveness in this area, using specific procedures that are described in the textbook, such as behavior rehearsal, role playing, coaching, cognitive restructuring, and so on. Practice with these procedures as a member first, so that you can get some idea of the values and applications of assertive-behavior training.

9. Working on specific goals. A real value of the behavioral approach is its specificity—its ability to translate broad goals into specific ones. State some broad goals that you'd like to attain. Then, in your group, practice making these goals concrete. Make them specific to the degree that you actually know what it is that you want and thus can measure or evaluate progress toward them. As a second part of this exercise, assume that members in one of your groups make global and vague state-

ments such as the following. Can you think of ways to make these goals clear and concrete?

a. "I'd like to be more spontaneous."

- Concrete goal is: _____

    _____

b. "I need to learn how to get in touch with my feelings."

- Concrete goal is: _____

    _____

c. "My goal is to become autonomous and an actualized person."

- Concrete goal is: _____

    _____

d. "There are a bunch of dumb fears I should get rid of."

- Concrete goal is: _____

    _____

e. "I'd like to be able to relate better."

- Concrete goal is: _____

    _____

f. "I'm all messed up, and I need a major overhaul."

- Concrete goal is: _____

    _____

g. "My goal is to get to know myself better."

- Concrete goal is: _____

    _____

10. <u>Groups designed for self-directed change</u>. Assume that you want to organize a group for people who are interested in self-directed change. For example, they may be interested in stopping smoking, taking weight off and keeping it off through a different diet and exercise program, or changing their habits of self-discipline regarding study or work. How would you design a group of this nature?

11. <u>Applying a self-directed program to yourself</u>. In your group or class, discuss the specific behavior that you want to work on during the semester. Next, decide what you are willing to do to change this behavior. Draw up a specific contract, and include details. (For instance, "I will lose ten pounds by the end of the semester, regulate eating habits, and ride a bicycle for an hour daily for the duration of the semester.") Then, during the remainder of the semester, practice your program and report your progress to your group. Ask a fellow student to support you if you get discouraged or find that you have difficulty sticking to your program. You can apply self-directed behavioral-modification methods to areas such as developing better patterns of organization, reducing stress through a program of meditation and relaxation exercises, changing what you consider to be negative behavior patterns, and so on.

12. <u>Cognitive restructuring in groups</u>. Identify a few major cognitions that have a negative impact on the way people behave. Think of common self-defeating statements that you have heard. Can you think of some methods for helping group members challenge negative cognitions and also develop a new and more effective set of beliefs and thoughts? Can you think of possible homework assignments to supplement the work done in the group sessions? What steps might you suggest to members in learning new ways of thinking?

13. <u>Self-reinforcement methods</u>. Behavioral group work teaches members how to reinforce themselves so that they are not dependent on external rewards to maintain newly acquired skills. In your class/group, experiment with ways you can <u>reinforce yourself</u> after successes. Brainstorm this topic in your group. Self-reinforcement may involve learning ways to praise yourself <u>and</u> at the same time remind yourself of certain realities that you tend to forget. An example of this is writing notes to yourself and putting them on the mirror. These notes could say "You are worthwhile," "I <u>am</u> enough," "I have a right to my own feelings," "I'll like myself better if I treat myself with regard," "I can take time for myself."

14. <u>Personal evaluation and critique of behavioral groups</u>. Discuss in your class/group what you consider to be the major strengths and weaknesses of the behavioral approach to groups. Consider such questions as:

- What learning principles apply to <u>all</u> groups?

- How can any group leader (regardless of theoretical orientation) draw on behavioral concepts and procedures?

- How would you feel about using behavioral techniques as a group leader?

- What are the limitations of behavior therapy?

- What are your criticisms?

14

RATIONAL–EMOTIVE GROUP THERAPY

PRECHAPTER PRIMER AND SELF-INVENTORY FOR
RATIONAL-EMOTIVE THERAPY

Directions: Refer to page 58 for general directions. Indicate your position on these statements, using the following code:

5 = I strongly agree with this statement.

4 = I agree, in most respects, with this statement.

3 = I am undecided in my opinion about this statement.

2 = I disagree, in most respects, with this statement.

1 = I strongly disagree with this statement.

_____ 1. It is primarily our beliefs that cause emotional disturbances;
            therefore, group work should focus on examining these beliefs.

_____ 2. For group leaders to be effective, they need to be willing to
            challenge, confront, and convince members to practice activities
            both inside and outside the group.

_____ 3. It is the group leader's task to show members how they have
            caused and now perpetuate their emotional/behavioral problems.

_____ 4. Group members have to be willing to discipline themselves by
            working hard both in and out of the group; they have to be
            active in confronting themselves.

_____ 5. A leader serves the role of a counterpropagandist.

_____ 6. A large part of the leader's task is to be a teacher, especially of how to detect and dispute irrational beliefs.

_____ 7. Homework assignments are a valuable part of group counseling.

_____ 8. Therapy is essentially a cognitive, active-directive, behavioral process.

_____ 9. A major function of the group leader is to serve as a model.

_____ 10. A warm and personal relationship between the group leader and the members is not essential to the group's success.

SUMMARY OF BASIC ASSUMPTIONS AND KEY CONCEPTS OF THE RATIONAL-EMOTIVE APPROACH

1. People's belief systems cause emotional disturbances. Situations alone do not determine emotional disturbances; rather, it is people's evaluations of these situations that are crucial.

2. People have a tendency to fall victim to irrational beliefs, and, although these beliefs were originally incorporated from external sources, people internalize and maintain these self-defeating beliefs by a process of self-indoctrination.

3. In order to overcome this indoctrination process that results in irrational thinking, group therapists use active-directive intervention methods, such as teaching, persuading, reindoctrinating, giving homework assignments, and so on to get group members to challenge their beliefs and substitute a rational belief system for an irrational one.

4. The member/leader relationship is not stressed; rather, what is emphasized is the group therapist's skill in challenging, confronting, and convincing the members to practice activities that will lead to positive change.

EXERCISES AND ACTIVITIES FOR THE RET APPROACH

Rationale

The rationale underlying most of these exercises and RET techniques is that most of us make irrational assumptions about ourselves and the world that lead to emotional/behavioral disturbances. The essence of RET is that rational thinking can lead to more effective living. To combat stubborn and persistent irrational beliefs, it is necessary to work and practice diligently and to replace faulty thinking with logical thinking.

The following activities and exercises are designed to help you experience the process of challenging your own thinking and to become aware of the consequent feelings of your belief system. As you work through these exercises on your own, with another person, and with a small group, think about ways that, as a group leader, you could incorporate them into group practice.

STAGES IN THE DEVELOPMENT OF THE RATIONAL-EMOTIVE THERAPY GROUP

Dimension	Initial Stage	Working Stage	Final Stage
Key developmental tasks and goals	Key task is to teach members the A-B-C theory of how they create and can "uncreate" their own disturbances, how they can detect their irrational beliefs and how they can attack these faulty beliefs. Members need to learn that situations themselves do not cause emotional problems; rather, their beliefs about these situations cause the problems. Thus, changing beliefs (not situations) is the road to improvement.	Group focuses on the identification and attacking of members' "musts," "shoulds," and "oughts." Members learn that, if life is not the way they want it to be, this may be unfortunate but not catastrophic. In place of self-defeating assumptions, members incorporate beliefs that are grounded in reality.	Ultimate aim is that participants internalize a rational philosophy of life, just as they internalized a set of irrational beliefs. This phase is one of reinforcement of new learning to replace old patterns. Emphasis is on teaching people better methods of self-management.
Role of group leader and tasks	Group leader shows members how they have caused their own misery by teaching them the connection between their emotional/behavioral disturbances and their beliefs.	Leader acts as a counterpropagandist who confronts members with the propaganda they originally accepted without question and with which they continue to indoctrinate themselves. Leader strives to modify members' thinking by challenging their underlying basic assumptions about reality.	Therapist continues to act as teacher by showing members methods of self-control, giving them homework assignments that involve active practice in real life, and correcting any lasting faulty patterns.
Role of group members	Members must be willing to discipline themselves and work hard, both during the sessions and between sessions. They must be active, both in and out of the group, for they learn by practicing and doing.	Members learn how to analyze, dispute, and debate by using scientific methods to question their belief systems. Members ask "What evidence supports my views?"	Group members integrate what they have learned and continue to make plans for how they can practice overcoming self-defeating thinking and emoting outside of the group.

Techniques	Educational methods: use of tapes, books, and lectures; suggestions; information giving; interpretation; group feedback and support; other active-directive, confrontational, didactic, philosophic, and action-oriented methods.	A rapid-fire and forceful set of techniques, which emphasize cognitive factors, is used. These include use of persuasion, homework assignments, desensitization, role playing, modeling and imitation, behavior rehearsal, operant control of thinking and emoting, group feedback and support, cognitive restructuring, and assertive training.	Continued use of emotive-evocative and cognitive behavioral techniques that people can use on their own after therapy terminates.
Questions to consider	What would you want to teach members about the ways they create their own disturbances? What are some common irrational beliefs that you might expect members to bring to a group? In what ways do you think a member's belief system is connected to how the person behaves and feels? How can you confront members to recognize their irrational thinking without adding to their defensiveness? What kind of relationship would you want to create with the members before you attempted to use forceful and directive procedures? What behavioral techniques would you employ in a RET group at the early stage?	To what degree have you recognized and challenged your own "musts," "shoulds," and oughts? To what extent have you looked at your self-defeating assumptions and self-defeating behavior? Do you agree that the role of leader is to act as a counter-propagandist who confronts members with beliefs they have accepted without thinking and questioning? What are some specific methods you might teach the members in learning how to analyze, dispute, and debate unexamined assumptions? What are some examples of RET homework that you are likely to use during the working stage? Can you keep from imposing your values upon members? Do you challenge them to think for themselves?	If you employ directive strategies and encourage members to take a specific course of action, are you clear about your own motives? Are you willing to state what your motivations are to your clients? Do you share with them your values that pertain to choices they might make? How can you teach members ways to maintain constructive thinking once they leave a group? How can you help members maintain gains they have made in challenging self-defeating attitudes? Might you want to integrate any other therapeutic techniques from other approaches during the final stages? If so, what? What are some ways that you could evaluate the effectiveness of your group as it moves toward termination?

Reactions: Summarize your reactions to the rational-emotive approach to group developmental stages. What do you like most? least? What aspects of this approach would you incorporate in your leadership style?

Exercises

1. Make a list of a few self-defeating sentences that you tend to say to yourself. The purpose of this exercise is for you to become aware of how <u>you</u> now continue to indoctrinate yourself with propaganda. Then take your self-defeating sentences and rewrite them in new and constructive ways, much like the example that follows:

   - <u>Self-defeating sentence</u>: "I'm sure I'll be a failure as a coun-selor."
   - <u>Constructive sentence</u>: "If I am willing to work diligently and apply myself to a good training program, then I'm sure that with experi-ence I'll succeed."

   - Self-defeating sentence: _____

     _____.

   - Constructive sentence: _____

     _____.

   - Self-defeating sentence: _____

     _____.

   - Constructive sentence: _____

     _____.

2. Write similar constructive sentences that you might suggest to a group member who repeated self-defeating sentences such as the following:

   - "I've always been stupid, and I suppose that I'll always be that way."

   - _____.

   - "I need to please everyone, because rejection is just terrible."

   - _____.

   - "Because my parents never really loved me, I guess nobody else could ever love me."

   - _____.

   - "Basically, I'm simply an irresponsible person."

   - _____.

3. <u>Self-rating</u>—giving yourself a "good" or "bad" evaluation based on your performances—can influence the way you think and feel. Ellis contends that the self-rating process constitutes one of the main sources of peo-

ple's emotional disturbances. Discuss these questions in class or in a small group.

  a. What are some of the ways you rate yourself?

  b. How do you _feel_ when you rate yourself critically?

4. <u>Homework assignments</u> are an integral part of RET group work. Think of your own patterns of behavior and ways that you'd like to think, feel, and behave more rationally. Then list a few specific homework assignments that you could do to challenge yourself to accomplish this. Carry out a few of these assignments, and bring the results to your group. Ask for suggestions from your fellow students/group members. Below are a couple of examples of homework assignments that may be useful to you.

  a. Do you have difficulties in making social contacts? Does it make you anxious to initiate a discussion with a member of the opposite sex? Do you want to feel more at ease in these situations than you do now? If so, try this experiment: Go to each of your classes early and sit in a different place each time near a person whom you don't know. Push yourself to initiate a conversation. Keep a record of all of the things, including irrational beliefs, you rehearse in your head before you make these contacts.

  b. Are you troubled by conflicts with authority figures? For example, would you like to feel easier about approaching an instructor to discuss your progress in the course? If so, what stops you from selecting at least one instructor and making the time and effort to discuss with him or her matters that are of importance to you?

5. Think of some in-group assignments or homework exercises for members who demonstrate problems such as the following, and write them down. Bring these assignments to class or group, and share ideas with one another.

  a. A woman says very little during the group sessions, because she's afraid that she'll sound stupid and that other members will laugh at her. One possible assignment is:

  _____

  _____

  _____

  b. A woman believes that men are always judging her in a critical fashion. She avoids men, both in the group and outside of it, because she doesn't want to feel negatively judged. One possible assignment is:

  _____

  _____

  _____

c. A young, unmarried man experiences a great deal of anxiety in asking women out on dates. Sometimes he'll avoid doing so, because he is afraid of being rejected or afraid of not knowing what to say to them if they accept. He'd like to overcome this avoidance behavior and lessen his anxiety. One possible assignment is:

_____

_____

_____

d. One of the members of a group you're leading tells you that he feels and believes that he must gain universal approval. When someone is displeased with him, he feels like a worm. Because of this he tries hard to figure out what every person in the group wants from him, and then he goes out of his way to meet these expectations. He says he is sick of being the "super nice guy" and desperately wants to change. One possible assignment is:

_____

_____

_____

e. A member describes her drive to be perfect and says that she carefully avoids situations and activities that make it difficult for her to feel that she's performed perfectly. She wants to relax and not be obsessed with the thought that she must be perfect in anything she attempts. One possible assignment is:

_____

_____

_____

6. Role playing with a cognitive focus can be useful in an RET group. Think of a situation that causes you difficulty—one that you'd be willing to share in your group or class—and role-play it. For example, you may feel victimized because you can't get your father's approval. Have a person play your role first, and you role-play your demanding father—the one who refuses to give approval no matter what is accomplished. After about five minutes or so, reverse roles: you be yourself while someone else plays your father as you portrayed him. Continue this for about another five minutes. Afterward, do a cognitive evaluation of this interchange in your group. Some questions you might include in your evaluation are:

  • How did you appear to others as you played yourself talking with your father?

  • Do you need his approval to survive?

- What will become of you if he never gives you his approval?

- What might you have to do to get his approval?

- How do you imagine you'd feel if you did what might be required to gain his acceptance?

- Can you gain self-acceptance, even if acceptance is not forthcoming from him?

- In what ways do you treat others like your father?

7. Imagine that you want to conduct an RET group in the agency or institution in which you work (or may someday work in the future). Convince your supervisor or the agency director of the advantages of doing RET in a group over doing it on an individual basis. What are some unique advantages of RET in groups, and why should your supervisor permit you to organize such a group? This can be a productive, as well as enjoyable, exercise that you can do in your group or class. Another student can play the role of the director/supervisor of the agency.

QUESTIONS FOR DISCUSSION AND EVALUATION

These questions can be used as a study guide as you read the corresponding chapter in the textbook, and they can provide discussion material for your class and small group.

1. Assume that you are leading a group and you confront a member with what you think is clearly an irrational assumption and a self-defeating view on her part. The member responds: "Look, I know that what I think is irrational. I know that all men aren't the bastard that my father was, and I keep telling myself this. Still, whenever I'm with a man, I feel that he's out to take advantage of me and that he's just like my father." How might you proceed with this member who recognizes that her belief is faulty yet can't seem to change her negative feelings?

2. Discuss how you think you'd function as an RET group counselor. RET is an active-directive, cognitive, behavioral, highly didactic method of therapy. Do you see any problems within yourself that might make it difficult for you to function in this manner? In your group or class, exchange ideas about specific aspects of RET that you'd find difficult to incorporate in your leadership style.

3. Do you think it is the group leader's place to teach the group members a philosophy of life? As a group leader, in challenging the belief systems of your clients, do you think that you can avoid imposing your values on them? Are there any values that you'd like to impose on the members of your groups? Do you think it is desirable to expose your values and beliefs to the group members? Do you think it is desirable to remain "value free" or "value neutral"? Discuss the reasons for your answers.

4. RET emphasizes cognitive processes. Do you think that enough attention is given to the emotional aspects of therapy? Do you think that self-defeating behavior can be eliminated exclusively by cognitive methods? Why or why not?

5. What dangers, if any, do you see for groups whose leaders function primarily within an RET perspective? Do you foresee any potentially harmful results that are more likely to occur with an RET approach than with less directive and active approaches?

15

REALITY THERAPY

PRECHAPTER PRIMER AND SELF-INVENTORY FOR
REALITY THERAPY

Directions: Refer to page 58 for general directions. Indicate your position on these statements, using the following code:

5 = I strongly agree with this statement.

4 = I agree, in most respects, with this statement.

3 = I am undecided in my opinion about this statement.

2 = I disagree, in most respects, with this statement.

1 = I strongly disagree with this statement.

_4_ 1. The group counselor's main task is to encourage the group members to face reality and make value judgments regarding present behavior.

_3_ 2. By emphasizing the unconscious, one avoids coming to grips with the issue of one's irresponsibility.

_4_ 3. Blaming others and making excuses for one's behavior leads to a cementing of one's identification with failure.

_4_ 4. Involvement is the core of therapy, for without it, there is no therapy.

_4_ 5. Group leaders should not focus on misery and failures; rather, they should accentuate the members' strengths.

STAGES IN THE DEVELOPMENT OF THE REALITY THERAPY GROUP

Dimension	Initial Stage	Working Stage	Final Stage
Key developmental tasks and goals	First task is to create member-to-member relationships and a sense of involvement in the group. Leader-to-member relationships based on trust are essential. Major goal of initial stage is to get members to look at the degree to which current behavior is meeting their needs.	Focus in on present behavior, rather than feelings. Past is important only insofar as it influences present behavior. The central goal is to create a climate wherein members will learn to understand how their irresponsibility and poor choices have led to their current personal problems; in this way, members can establish "success" identity.	Specific plans for achieving desirable behavior patterns must be established; although plans are crucial for behavioral change to occur, a noncritical therapeutic milieu must be created in order to give members the strength to carry out their plans.
Role of group leader and tasks	Group leader has the task of fostering involvement among the members; he or she encourages involvement by being active and involved with every member. Leader may question, asks others to make comments, and encourage interaction in the group. Modeling is crucial. Leader focuses on current behavior and begins to get the members to look at what they are getting from their behavior.	Leader encourages members to evaluate their own behavior, asks members whether their current behavior is meeting their needs, and firmly rejects excuses and rationalizations. Counselor praises and approves responsible behavior. Counselor avoids labeling people, with diagnostic categories.	Leader assists members in formulating realistic plans for change and creates a noncritical therapeutic climate that helps members believe that change is possible. Leader does not give up, even if members fail to carry out plans; he or she insists on finding a short-range plan that will lead to success.
Role of group members	Members focus on current behavior and problem areas. Focus may be on how each member attempts to gain love and feelings of self-worth and success. Members are expected to face their problems and to make plans to solve them. Making these plans for change begins early in the group.	Members evaluate own behavior and make value judgments about this behavior. They must understand what they are doing as well as what they are getting from this behavior. Members must decide for themselves if they are willing to change their patterns of behavior.	Realistic plans to change behavior must be made and carried out. If members do not carry out their plans, they are expected to state when they will complete them. They are to accept responsibility for what they do.

Techniques	In keeping with the goal of establishing involvement, leader will encourage members to talk about any subjects of interest to them. An attempt is made to find out what members want from the group and contracts are typically developed early in the group.	Confrontation; insistance on importance of evaluating behavior and making decisions; avoidance of punishment.	Contracts; behavioral strategies, such as role playing, behavior rehearsal, homework assignments, and so on; encouragement and support.
Questions to consider	Once you have established a relationship with members, you will want to focus on current behavior. In doing so, questions you may want to ask are: • What are you doing now? • What did you do this week? • What did you want to do differently this past week? • What stopped you from doing what you wanted to do? • What will you do tomorrow? If your members seem reluctant to accept the responsibility for their own problems, what might you do? How can you teach acceptance of responsibility? What use might you make of contracts? How would you help members establish clear and realistic goals? Would you focus exclusively on behavioral goals? Would you work with feelings and thoughts as well as current behavior?	A central task is to get members to look at what they are doing to decide whether their course of action is working. How can you challenge members in a nonjudgmental way to make an evaluation of their behavior? How can you avoid lecturing and imposing your values on members? How can you challenge members to make an honest evaluation if they seem resistant? What if the members cling to what you consider self-defeating ways of behaving? What do you see as your role in planning with members, checking with them about how well the plan is working, and making revisions in plans as needed? How can you use the group process in helping members make and follow through with their commitments?	How might you avoid giving up on certain members, even if they fail to meet their commitments? What might you do with members who do not seem willing to carry out short-range plans? What are some ways that you might use the group sessions to help members practice new behaviors that they will try out in daily situations? What methods might you employ to encourage members to practice outside the group what they are learning in the session? What are some ways you might help members express and explore their fears of failing? How can you reinforce success and small gains? Can you think of ways to encourage members to take action, even though they feel defeated? What follow-up procedures might you use to assess the extent to which members make and maintain positive changes after a group?

Reactions: Summarize your reactions to the reality-therapy perspective on group developmental stages. What do you like most? least? What aspects of this approach would you incorporate in your leadership style?

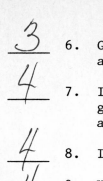

 3   6. Group work should aim to change behavior, rather than feelings or attitudes.

 4   7. It is not the group leader's role to make value judgments for group members; rather, he or she should challenge them to evaluate their own behavior.

 4   8. Insight is <u>not</u> essential to produce change.

 4   9. Unless clients are willing to accept responsibility for their behavior, they will not be able to change their behavior.

 4 10. <u>Responsibility</u> implies meeting one's own needs in such a way that other people are not deprived of fulfilling their needs.

SUMMARY OF BASIC ASSUMPTIONS AND KEY CONCEPTS OF THE REALITY-THERAPY APPROACH

1. We all have a need to develop a "success" identity, and one way of doing this is by living realistically and accepting responsibility for our behavior.

2. We perceive the world against the background of our needs, rather than seeing it the way it is in reality. We create our own inner world. Behavior is the attempt to control our perceptions of the external world to fit our internal and personal world.

3. Group leaders using reality therapy tend to focus on what members can do now to change their behavior—being willing to make a commitment to change, developing a plan for action, and following through. Thus, group therapists do not explore the past, and they do not accept any excuses for the failure of members to follow through with their commitments.

4. Like behavior therapy, this approach is basically active, directive, and didactic, and it employs a contract method. The group therapist's main task is to encourage the members to face reality and make value judgments regarding present behavior. Thus, behavior is the focus, rather than insight, or one's past or unconscious motivations.

EXERCISES AND ACTIVITIES FOR THE REALITY-THERAPY APPROACH

Rationale

Some of the following exercises, activities, and questions can be used on your own, and others can be used in small groups. After you have worked with this material and answered the questions, you will be in a better position to know which of these ideas you might want to employ in the groups you lead or will lead.

Exercises

1. Responsibility

   a. Accepting responsibility is a major goal of reality therapy. What is your own view of responsibility? How, specifically, were you taught responsibility?

   b. Talk about how responsible you are right now in your life. What are some ways in which you may attempt to dodge responsibility. How do you accept it?

   c. Do you blame others for the way you see yourself? In what ways do you attempt to put responsibility on external factors to justify the way you are? What would it be like to you to fully accept the responsibility for the way you are?

2. "Success" and "failure" identities

   a. How does what you say about yourself affect the way people view and treat you? What self-fulfilling prophecies do you subject yourself to? In what ways do you set yourself up for success or failure?

   b. If your parents were to describe you in terms of a success/failure identity, what might they say about you? What do you imagine your best friend would say? If you are in a group now, how do you think other members might perceive you?

   c. Is there a difference between the way you see yourself now and the way you'd like to be? If so, what changes would you like to make? In what ways do you restrict your possibilities by rigidly adhering to fixed notions that do not allow for change? Do you tell yourself that you can't be other than you are—that you can't change?

3. Value judgment and self-evaluation. What are some values that are important to you? What difficulties do you, as a group leader, predict that you'll have as a result of value clashes with group members? What kinds of client would you have difficulty working with in a group because of a divergence in philosophy, life-style, and value system.

4. Involvement. Do you think the group leader should become involved with the participants? Why or why not? How would you involve yourself in your groups? With what clients would you most easily become involved? With what people would it be difficult for you to become involved?

5. Developing a plan for change

   a. What commitments would you, as a leader, expect from those who participated in your groups? What methods would you use to assist them in formulating specific action plans? How do you imagine that you'd handle participants who continually made plans but then returned to group without having followed through on most of them?

   b. How would you, as a group member, deal with group members who talked about wanting to change but refused to make any concrete plans to put into action outside the group. Perhaps they would insist that they had never been able to make plans. What would you tell them?

QUESTIONS FOR DISCUSSION AND EVALUATION

1. The main task of the group leader, according to Glasser, is to encourage group members to face reality and to judge their own behavior and evaluate its consequences. In carrying out this task, counselors can't avoid getting involved with members in the realm of values and morality. This involvement raises a number of questions.

    a. What is reality? Who defines reality—society? the counselor? the client? What if the client has a different view of reality than the counselor? How do cross-cultural factors fit in here?

    b. As a counselor, what are your criteria for judging what is acceptable and realistic behavior? Again, how are cultural factors related to your answer?

    c. How might you, as a group counselor, work with a group of adolescents who refused to evaluate their behavior and who maintained that the only thing they wanted was to be released from the institution where they had been sent by the judge.

    d. What problems might exist for you if the members of your group had a radically different background and different life-style from yours? Can you enter the world of reality of clients who have a life-style sharply divergent from your own?

2. Glasser maintains that counselors are not moralists, though he recognizes the exploration of morality is a vital part of the counseling process. He maintains that counselors should teach clients that the key to finding happiness is to accept responsibility for making their own evaluations. Glasser's position raises some central ethical questions, such as:

    a. How fine is the line between merely challenging clients to assess their behavior and actively teaching them what they should value?

    b. Do you think it's appropriate for a group counselor to talk openly about his or her values? Might this lead the members to incorporate the counselor's values, rather than developing their own values?

    c. Or do you think it's better for counselors to keep their values "out of the counseling process"? Is this possible? Are there times when a group leader might want to <u>impose</u> certain values on the group instead of merely exposing these values? When? Why or why not?

3. What are the advantages and the limitations of reality therapy's strict emphasis on present behavior to the exclusion of exploring the client's past?

4. Reality therapy focuses on current behavior, not on insight, feelings, and attitudes. Do you agree that insight is <u>not</u> a prerequisite for change? Why or why not? Do you think that, if people change their <u>behavior</u> in constructive ways, they will automatically change their <u>feel</u>-

ings? Is it necessary to change one's <u>attitude</u> before effectively changing one's behavior?

5. Glasser believes that the group leader should provide a model for group members to emulate. Do you agree? How could you decide whether the model you provide is worth emulating?

6. Glasser says that it's important for the group leader to focus on the members' strengths and assets in counseling, as opposed to dwelling on their problems and shortcomings. What advantages and limitations do you see in this? How might focusing on group members' strengths and positive qualities help them formulate realistic plans for change and follow through with these plans?

7. According to Glasser, the notion of transference provides a way for therapists and group members to hide; it prevents <u>real</u> involvement from developing between the client and the counselor. Do you agree with this view? If you agree, how do you think this would affect your style of leading a group?

8. Like transference, the unconscious is given little attention in reality therapy, in order to avoid giving clients excuses to avoid facing reality. Do you agree with this stance? What would be the advantages and disadvantages of emphasizing only conscious processes during group work?

9. Commitment is an essential part of reality therapy. As a group counselor how might you assist people with a "failure" identity who have trouble making and keeping the commitments necessary for change?

PART THREE

Application and Integration

ILLUSTRATION OF A GROUP IN ACTION:
VARIOUS PERSPECTIVES

GUIDELINES FOR CRITIQUING VARIOUS
APPROACHES TO GROUP THERAPY

The textbook's illustration of a group in action is designed to give you a general picture of how different group-counseling approaches could be applied to the same group. Thus, it gives you practical examples of the advantages and disadvantages of each approach. In your class or group, using the following questions as a guide, discuss what aspects you like best (and least) about each approach as it was presented in the textbook illustration. Then explore the ways to integrate several approaches in your own leadership style—to selectively borrow concepts and procedures from all of the therapies—and to begin developing your own theory of group counseling.

Using the Psychoanalytic Approach

1. How could the group leader create a sense of trust in this group?

2. How would the members' resistance be explained? How might resistance be handled by the leader?

3. How could the leader work with any strong feelings that the members directed against him or her?

4. What would the group leader primarily focus on in this group?

5. At what stage of a group's development do you think psychoanalytic concepts and techniques are most suitable? What would you most want to incorporate in your style from this approach?

Using the Adlerian Approach

1. How would an Adlerian go about getting early recollections from members, and how would these memories be used in the group?

2. What possibilities can you see in using the group as a way to re-create the original family of the members? What are some ways that work with the family constellation could proceed in a group context?

3. Adlerians are interested in the personal goals of members, including a focus on what they are working toward and what kind of life they want. Applied to the group described in the chapter, how might a leader work with member goals?

4. At what stage of a group's development do you think Adlerian concepts and techniques are most appropriate? What concepts and techniques would you want to draw from in this approach?

Using the Psychodrama Approach

1. How could the group leader "warm up" the group? (Would you use any of these techniques in your group work?)

2. What value would the group leader place on reenacting past events or enacting anticipated situations? (What do psychodrama and psychoanalytic approach have in common? How do they differ?)

3. How could the group leader work with relationship conflicts?

4. At what stage of a group's development would psychodrama procedures be most effective? What do you want to take from this approach?

Using the Existential Approach

1. What could the group leader focus on in this group? (What would you focus on?)

2. How might the theme "I'm alive, but I feel dead" be explained and dealt with?

3. How would the group leader describe this group and explain the occurrences in it, as opposed to the description of a group leader using the psychoanalytic approach?

4. How could the group leader deal with group members who found little meaning in life and who expressed suicidal thoughts? (How would you deal with these issues as a group leader?)

5. At what stage of a group's development would this approach be most appropriate?

Using the Person-Centered Approach

1. How would the leader attempt to create trust?

2. How could the group leader work with a member who expressed problems with loneliness?

3. How could the leader provide more direction? (Do you think this group or any particular members in it <u>need</u> more direction and structure than is illustrated?)

4. At what stage of a group's development might this approach be of the most value? What do you want to draw upon from the approach?

Using the Gestalt Approach

1. How might the group leader work with the members of this group, as contrasted with the way a person-centered group leader would work?

2. If a member in this group wanted to work on a dream that related to emptiness, how would the leader carry this out—as opposed to the way a psychoanalytic group leader would work? (Which method would you tend to use, and why?)

3. Would the group leader use many action-oriented therapeutic techniques? Why or why not?

4. Would the group leader focus mainly on experiencing moment-to-moment feelings? (How much emphasis do you think should be put on the cognitive aspects of a group therapy?)

5. At what stage of a group's development do you see Gestalt as being most useful and appropriate?

Using Transactional Analysis

1. How would the TA leader—as opposed to a psychoanalytic leader—work with a member's drinking problem?

2. Contracts will be made between the leader and the members. How do you think contracts will work in this group?

3. How could the group leader also draw on Gestalt techniques to obtain the maximum benefits for this group?

4. What role would examining old decisions and making new ones play in this group's work?

5. At what stage of a group's development do you think TA is most useful? What concepts and techniques do you want to use from TA?

Using the Behavioral Approach

1. How would the group leader begin the group? (What are the typical steps and sequences in the behavioral group?)

2. How would the leader work with this group— as contrasted with a psychoanalytic leader? an existential leader? a Gestalt leader?

3. What learning principles would the group leader employ in this group? (Discuss key learning principles such as reinforcement, modeling, feedback, and so on.)

4. How could the group leader work with a member who is very unassertive? (How would you work with such a problem?)

5. At what stage of a group would behavioral methods be most appropriate? Which of these methods are you most likely to use in your leading?

Using the Rational-Emotive Approach

1. The techniques employed in group work will be directive and confrontational. Do you think such techniques could be effective in this group? Why or why not? (Would you be comfortable using these techniques in your own group?)

2. How could the group leader also draw on Gestalt techniques to obtain the maximum benefits for this group?

3. How might the leader deal with the member who fears rejection? (How would this differ from what the person-centered therapist would do?)

4. How could the leader deal with the member with a marriage problem? (How would this differ from what an RET therapist would do? what a leader using psychodrama would do?)

5. At what stage in a group would RET be most appropriate? What might you take from RET and use in your style of leading?

Using Reality Therapy

1. How would the group leader respond to a member who has blamed his past for his current problems?

2. How could the leader get members to evaluate their current behavior? What if the members gave excuses? (What do you think of the role assumed by the reality therapist? Would it fit you? Why or why not?)

3. In what ways would the reality-therapy leader assist members in formulating a plan for action? How is what one is doing in the present related to making plans for change and committing oneself to this program?

4. At what stage in the group's development would reality therapy be particularly appropriate? What concepts and procedures might you borrow from this approach for incorporation in your style of leading?

SUMMARY EXERCISE

After you've thought about and discussed the above questions, attempt to sort out your theoretical preferences. Which of these therapeutic approaches appeal to you the most, and why? What specific aspects of each model would you want to incorporate in your own personal style of leadership? What possibilities do you see for blending several approaches, especially at the various stages in a group's development. Think about the timing of using techniques from each of the approaches. Which techniques would you want to use in the beginning, middle, and ending stages in the development of a group? Discuss with fellow students the basic features of your own personalized theoretical orientation.

17

COMPARISONS, CONTRASTS, AND INTEGRATION

QUESTIONS FOR DISCUSSION AND EVALUATION

Perspectives on Goals for Group Counseling

1. How does the theoretical orientation of a group practitioner influence the group's goals and the direction it takes? How can a leader's values and beliefs influence the direction of the group?

2. In view of the many differences among the various theoretical approaches to group therapy, how is it possible for there to be a common ground among behavioral-oriented groups and experiential- and relationship-oriented groups? How can long-range goals and concrete short-term goals be integrated into group practice?

3. As a group leader, what value would you place on the freedom of members to select personal goals? How would you bring the members' goals and the goals you have for the group into agreement? What problems can you foresee if these goals do not agree?

4. How do a group's goals relate to its type of membership?

5. Consult the overview chart of group-therapy goals in the text. After you review these goals, complete the following list. In your own words, state what you consider to be the central goal of each of these models:

    a. Psychoanalytic: _____

    _____

b. Adlerian: _____

_____

c. Psychodrama: _____

_____

d. Existential: _____

_____

e. Person-centered: _____

_____

f. Gestalt: _____

_____

g. TA: _____

_____

h. Behavior therapy: _____

_____

i. RET: _____

_____

j. Reality therapy: _____

_____

Which model comes closest to your thinking? Which model do you disagree
with most strongly? As you review the models, determine which goals
you'd choose to incorporate in your own group-counseling theory.

Role and Functions of the Group Leader

1. In the text, review the chart that summarizes the role and function of
    the group leader in the various theoretical approaches. Then give a one-
    sentence description of what you think is the central role/function of
    the leader from the point of view of each of these models.

    a. Psychoanalytic: _____

    _____

    b. Adlerian: _____

    _____

c. Psychodrama: _____

_____

d. Existential: _____

_____

e. Person-centered: _____

_____

f. Gestalt: _____

_____

g. TA: _____

_____

h. Behavior therapy: _____

_____

i. RET: _____

_____

j. Reality therapy: _____

_____

2. After reviewing your summary above, write down the specific roles and functions that you think you will perform as a group leader.

_____

_____

_____

_____

3. If you were asked in a job interview to describe in one sentence what you considered your central role as a group leader to be, what would you say?

_____

_____

_____

_____

4. Review the different stages in the development of a group. How do the group leader's roles change during these stages?

The Issue of Structuring and the Division of Responsibility

1. It is clear that a group leader will provide <u>structure</u> for the group. What is <u>not</u> predetermined is the <u>degree</u> and <u>kind</u> of structure he or she provides. The group could range from being extremely unstructured (the person-centered group) to being highly structured and directive (behavioral group). Review the chart in the textbook on degree of structuring and division of responsibility. Which theories come closest to your view? Why? What theories do you disagree with? Why? How could you combine some of these different approaches to structuring a group? How can these models stimulate your thinking regarding what type and degree of structuring you want to provide a group? <u>How does structuring relate to the group's stage of development</u>?

2. <u>The division of responsibility</u>, like structuring, can differ widely according to the theoretical approach used in a group. Some therapies place primary responsibility on the group leader for the direction and outcome of the group. Other therapies give primary responsibility to the group members and tend to downplay the role of the leader. What is your position on this matter?

3. The group leader must always maintain a balance between taking on too much responsibility for the group and denying any responsibility for its direction. What problems do you foresee for a group if the leader assumes either too much or not enough responsibility?

4. Review the chart in the textbook on the division of responsibility, and then give a one-sentence summary of the position taken by each of these models:

a. Psychoanalytic: _____

_____

b. Adlerian: _____

_____

c. Psychodrama: _____

_____

d. Existential: _____

_____

e. Person-centered: _____

_____

f. Gestalt: _____

   _____

g. TA: _____

   _____

h. Behavior therapy: _____

   _____

i. RET: _____

   _____

j. Reality therapy: _____

   _____

5. What does each of the above therapeutic approaches to responsibility of-
    fer to you as a group practitioner? Would you, as a group leader, want
    to assume more responsibility at some stages of a group than at others.
    How might your degree of responsibility differ at the beginning, middle,
    and ending stages of a group's development?

Group Leader's Use of Technique

1. Review the chart in the textbook on group-therapy techniques. Then
    write down the specific technique(s) from each theory that you find
    most useful.

   a. Psychoanalytic: _____

      _____

   b. Adlerian: _____

      _____

   c. Psychodrama: _____

      _____

   d. Existential: _____

      _____

   e. Person-centered: _____

      _____

f. Gestalt: _____

_____

g. TA: _____

_____

h. Behavior therapy: _____

_____

i. RET: _____

_____

j. Reality therapy: _____

_____

2. Which techniques will you select and combine to use when you lead a
    group? How can each of these techniques be adapted to lead different
    kinds of group? Write down the techniques that you think best fit the
    kind of person you are; keep in mind techniques you'd be likely to use
    at the initial, transition, working, and final stages of a group.

_____

_____

_____

_____

_____

_____

_____

3. In small groups discuss some of the following questions pertaining to
    your views on the use of techniques as a group leader. Focus on those
    techniques that seem most suited to your personality and leadership
    style, and pay attention to the particular stage in the evolution of a
    group. At what stage of a group are you likely to use certain tech-
    niques; at what point in a group's development might you be inclined
    not to use certain techniques? Why?

    a. From each of the ten theories, which techniques appeal to you the
        most?

    b. Can you give reasons for using the techniques you choose?

c. Do you believe that the use of techniques can enhance or interfere with group process? In what way might techniques have either effect?

d. To what degree are you inclined to use structured or planned techniques in a group? At what stage of a group's history? For what purposes?

e. Do you agree that techniques are no less significant to group process than the group leader's personality and the relationship he or she has with group members? Explain.

f. To what extent might you rely on the use of techniques to give direction to a session? What are some examples of these techniques you might use to provide direction?

g. Should clients be informed about the purpose of the techniques you use? What might you tell members about a given technique?

Toward a Synthesis of Theories Applied to Practice

Review the sections of the chapter in the textbook that deal with developing an integrated eclectic model of group counseling. Strive to begin developing your own synthesis of theories applied to groups at the various stages of development. I suggest that you use the questions below as the basis for discussion in small groups. With your fellow students, think of ways to develop a conceptual framework that can account for the factors of cognition, emotion, and behavior. Also, focus on various theoretical approaches that you'd probably draw upon at each of the stages in the life history of a group. Strive for a blending and an integration of theories that will provide you with a cognitive map to explain what goes on in a group as it evolves.

1. What general group-process goals would guide your interventions at the initial, transition, working, and final stages of a group? How might the goals for a group differ with respect to the period of development?

2. How would you describe your major role and functions at each of the stages of a group? What changes, if any, do you see in your leadership functions at the various phases?

3. What kind of structuring do you most want to provide at each of the phases of a group's development? How would you describe the division of responsibility (between you as leader and the members) at each of the stages?

4. In terms of techniques in the facilitation of group process at the various phases of development, what possible integration can you come up with? How can you combine theories and techniques to work on the three levels of feeling/thinking/doing? (For example, can you think of ways to combine experiential techniques with cognitive and behavioral methods? What ways might you blend Gestalt or psychodrama methods with RET or behavioral techniques?)

5. During the pregroup stage, how could you draw upon those approaches that stress therapeutic contracts? How might you help members formulate a contract during the screening and orientation interview?

6. During the _initial_ stage, can you think of aspects of the relationship-oriented approaches (especially the existential and person-centered approaches) that you could use as a basis for building trust among the members and between yourself and the members? How might you look to the behavioral approaches in assisting members to develop specific personal goals?

7. During the _transition_ stage, how might you understand resistance from a psychoanalytic and an Adlerian perspective? How could you work with resistance by using the group as a way to re-create the members' original family? Can you think of theories you could draw upon that would help you work with members from a feeling/thinking/behaving perspective when a group is in transition?

8. During the _working_ stage, what kind of integration of theoretical perspectives will allow you to bring a complete approach into focus that considers the feeling/thinking/behaving dimensions? How much emphasis would you be inclined to place on the expression of emotion? How much focus would you place on what members are thinking and how their cognitions influence their behavior? What are some examples of techniques you'd employ to work on a behavioral level? Can you think of ways in which you might use role-playing, behavior-rehearsal, and feedback techniques? What are some ways you can think of to promote interaction among the members? How could you link the work of several members together? What are some ways to develop themes in a group that many members are able to work with at the same time?

9. During the _final_ stage, how could you borrow strategies from the cognitive, behavioral therapies to help members in their task of consolidating their learnings and applying them to life outside of the group? What are some examples of ways in which you might help members practice new learning and apply it to social situations in daily life? What are some ways of teaching members how to create support systems once they leave a group?

10. At the _postgroup_ stage, how could you apply behavioral strategies for accountability and evaluation purposes? What specific follow-up procedures would you want for the groups you lead?

    Note: Now that you have addressed the questions above, attempt to develop your own questions on the applications of theory to group practice, and look toward your own personal synthesis. Explain how you see groups from a developmental perspective, giving emphasis to those theories that most help you understand how groups function.

TO THE OWNER OF THIS BOOK

We hope that you have enjoyed the Manual for Theory and Practice of Group Counseling (second edition). We'd like to know as much about your experiences with the manual as possible. Only through your comments and the comments of others can we learn how to make the manual a better book for future readers.

School: _____   Your Instructor's Name: _____

1. What I like most about this manual is: _____

_____

_____

2. What I like least about this manual is: _____

_____

_____

3. Specific suggestions for improving the manual are: _____

_____

4. Some ways in which I used this manual in class were: _____

_____

5. Some ways in which I used this manual out of class were: _____

_____

6. Some of the manual's exercises that were used most meaningfully in my

class were: _____

_____

7. My general reaction to this manual is: _____

8. In the space below or in a separate letter, please write any other comments about the book you'd like to make. We welcome your suggestions!

_____

_____

_____

9. Please write down the name of the course in which you used this manual:

_____

Optional:

Your Name: _____ Date: _____

May Brooks/Cole quote you, either in promotion for the <u>Manual for Theory and Practice of Group Counseling</u> or in future publishing ventures?

Yes _____ No _____

                                        Sincerely,

                                        Gerald Corey

FOLD HERE

FOLD HERE

                                        FIRST CLASS
                                        Permit No. 84
                                        Monterey, CA

BUSINESS REPLY MAIL
No Postage Necessary if Mailed in United States

Dr. Gerald Corey
Brooks/Cole Publishing Company
Monterey, CA 93940